Selling Your House Without a Broker

Selling Your House Without a Broker

The Complete Guide to Saving Thousands of Dollars in Commissions by Selling Your Own Home

Dale Chaney and Mary Beth Libbey

CONTEMPORARY
BOOKS, INC.
CHICAGO ■ NEW YORK

Library of Congress Cataloging-in-Publication Data

Chaney, Dale.
  Selling your house without a broker.

  1. House selling.   I. Libbey, Mary Beth.   II. Title.
HD1379.C48   1986   333.33'8   86-24043
ISBN 0-8092-4833-6

Affordability tables, prorating table, and real estate sales
contract reprinted with permission from Chicago Title
Insurance Company.

Published by Contemporary Books, Inc.
180 North Michigan Avenue, Chicago, Illinois 60601
Manufactured in the United States of America
Library of Congress Catalog Card Number: 86-24043
International Standard Book Number: 0-8092-4833-6

Published simultaneously in Canada by Beaverbooks, Ltd.
195 Allstate Parkway, Valleywood Business Park
Markham, Ontario L3R 4T8 Canada

Contents

1
The Gain and the Goal

What do you stand to gain by selling your house without a broker? You can keep the broker's sales commission, get a better price for your house, and make a quicker sale.

What's the down side to selling your house without a broker? You can suffer the inconvenience of a long, drawn-out sales effort, end up taking a lower price for your house, and, perhaps, even fail and have to turn to a broker to sell your house. If so, you lose all the money you spent on your futile marketing attempt.

What makes the difference? Basically, the outcome depends on how well you understand the things a broker does and how well you do those things for yourself.

A BROKER'S DUTIES

Real estate brokers act as intermediaries between buyer and seller. They provide a range of services from advising you on ways to increase the value of your house, to setting the price, to marketing your house, to showing it and getting the offer. In addition, good brokers will qualify your

1

buyer, help your buyer find financing, negotiate a sales contract, and supervise other details of the sale.

Though it may sound like a big job (and it can be), there isn't anything that a real estate broker does for a commission that you can't do for yourself. In some cases, you can do it more effectively.

Real estate brokers commonly want a listing contract of at least ninety days, which means you give them the exclusive opportunity and three months in which to sell your home. But they may not aggressively show your house for all ninety days. In practice, what can happen is the broker will bring a whirlwind of prospects in during the first two weeks of the listing contract. If you don't get a suitable offer out of it in that time, your house may not get much action for the next couple of months—which is valuable marketing time lost—and then during the last two weeks of the contract the broker will bring in another whirlwind of prospects, just to convince you to renew the listing contract for another ninety days. It doesn't always happen this way, and there are many fine brokers operating in the industry, but it does happen.

You may be able to accomplish a quicker sale than a broker could, so long as you learn the broker's job.

When real estate brokers price your property, they may peg it at the low end of a reasonable range. The reason is simple. They deal in volume, and if a lower price will move your house faster, then they will pressure you to take a lower price. Without a broker, you may be able to get a better price for your house because you are acting in your own self-interest and not merely looking for a quick sale at a low price.

And, regardless of how long they take to sell it or how low the selling price, you're still obligated to pay a sales commission. If you sell on your own, you may also keep the sales commission for yourself, or keep at least part of it, depending on your pricing strategy.

THE SALES COMMISSION

Despite some slight variation, commission rates tend to be so uniform that many people believe they are set by law or local real estate boards. In fact, rates are set by each firm individually. Thus, theoretically, you could negotiate to a lower selling fee, though in practice it is seldom possible. Few brokers will budge on their price, though some may offer reduced services for a reduced fee.

To help you calculate your potential gain by selling your house without a broker, refer to the table of commissions.

Of course, your broker doesn't get the whole commission. At best, she (about 80 percent of brokers are women) or he will keep half of the total with the other half going to the broker's agent. This split is based on the assumption that your broker not only had your listing but also supplied the buyer. At worst, your broker will keep only one-fourth of the total, if another broker brought in the buyer. The other three-fourths would be divided evenly among the buyer's broker, that broker's agent, and your broker's agent. So, on a $100,000 house, a broker will make anywhere from $1,500 to $3,000 in commissions. Considering these figures, a broker may sell as much as $1,000,000 in property and get only $20,000 in commissions. That explains why they commonly take the volume approach to house selling.

WHAT'S YOUR GAIN?

If you get stuck with paying the whole commission, it doesn't come out of your sales price, it comes out of your profit. If your house sells for $100,000, and after paying off your mortgage and any closing costs (see Chapter 12) you have a net profit of, say, $50,000, that $6,000 commission suddenly becomes 12 percent of your profit.

So, when you figure what you have to gain by selling your house without a broker, judge the gain by its effect on your potential profit.

Of course, it's hard to calculate how many dollars in sales commissions you will keep, because there are many variables. What kind of marketing tools—newspapers, magazines—are you going to use, and how much do they cost? How long will you have to run your ads? What will your pricing strategy be? Do you want to sell quickly, or do you want to hang in there for top dollar? Are you willing to

BROKER COMMISSIONS
(6% of Sales Price)

Sale Price	Commission	Sale Price	Commission
$50,000	$3,000	$86,000	$5,160
51,000	3,060	87,000	5,220
52,000	3,120	88,000	5,280
53,000	3,180	89,000	5,340
54,000	3,240	90,000	5,400
55,000	3,300	91,000	5,460
56,000	3,360	92,000	5,520
57,000	3,420	93,000	5,580
58,000	3,480	94,000	5,640
59,000	3,540	95,000	5,700
60,000	3,600	96,000	5,760
61,000	3,660	97,000	5,820
62,000	3,720	98,000	5,880
63,000	3,780	99,000	5,940
64,000	3,840	100,000	6,000
65,000	3,900	101,000	6,060
66,000	3,960	102,000	6,120
67,000	4,020	103,000	6,180
68,000	4,080	104,000	6,240
69,000	4,140	105,000	6,300
70,000	4,200	106,000	6,360
71,000	4,260	107,000	6,420
72,000	4,320	108,000	6,480
73,000	4,380	109,000	6,540
74,000	4,440	110,000	6,600
75,000	4,500	111,000	6,660
76,000	4,560	112,000	6,720
77,000	4,620	113,000	6,780
78,000	4,680	114,000	6,840
79,000	4,740	115,000	6,900
80,000	4,800	116,000	6,960
81,000	4,860	117,000	7,020
82,000	4,920	118,000	7,080
83,000	4,980	119,000	7,140
84,000	5,040	120,000	7,200
85,000	5,100	121,000	7,260

do some quick upgrading on your property before putting it on the market?

Ultimately, you may want to figure your return on an hourly basis. As a worst-case scenario, assume your house sells for $50,000 and you committed one-hundred hours to selling it. The broker's commission would have been $3,000, so you earned about $30 an hour for selling it yourself. If circumstances were more favorable and you committed only ten hours to doing the things a broker would do, you earned about $300 an hour—not bad for a day's work. Indeed, the authors spent approximately ten hours on marketing and showing their house and not only sold their house for their target price, but kept the entire sales commission.

To estimate how much time you will have to commit to the project, you'll need to know more about the job ahead. Depending on your goals and strategy, how fast houses are moving in your market, and how well you handle the sales and administrative aspects of the job, it could take you from ten hours to one-hundred hours or more (spread over the length of the process).

The goal, certainly, is to sell as quickly as possible for the highest price possible.

YOUR GAIN—BROKER'S LOSS

One of your first and biggest challenges in collecting your gain is resisting brokers' efforts to list your house. After all, your gain is their loss. They will be among the first to respond to lawn signs and classified ads that declare *For Sale by Owner*. When they call, they will hit you with many horror stories, maybe all true, about FSBO (pronounced fiz-bo and short for "For Sale by Owner") failures. They will give you facts and figures to illustrate the odds against you. Don't ignore them. Listen to them, because they're telling you what will happen if you don't understand what you're doing.

They have other, more low-key approaches. One is a mail program aimed at FSBOs. After the broker's initial phone contact, the firm sends cards every other day for ten days, hitting you during the first two weeks you are trying to sell your own house. So, hold off on putting your house on the market until you've learned the background material (by reading this book).

Brokers know what to say to get sellers interested. For example, there's the climbing-interest-rate technique. They don't try to scare you with it—not exactly—they just mention that money is getting tight and that buyers will need higher incomes to make monthly payments. Therefore, qualified buyers are getting a bit harder to find, and that's their specialty. They can find you a qualified buyer.

Some will try to snare you with the possibility that they can get a higher price for you—suggesting the possibility that you may be underpricing your house. Brokers will usually ask you what you think you can sell the house for. That gives them some idea of where you stand. They will generally talk about a price range, but before they give the range, they try to get your price estimate. They don't want to dig themselves a hole by blurting out a price or even a range, because they don't know if another broker has given you a higher selling estimate already.

Others will sell their services, using a series of "can you" questions to undermine your confidence in dealing with some necessary details—which actually will be handled by your attorney. Can you qualify your buyer? Can you help the buyer get financing? Can you see the thing through closing? And so on.

Of course, their motivation is to get you to list with them, and they will press for an appointment. They will be reluctant to give you many constructive facts over the telephone and will want to come over and talk with you in person. In general, tell them "No," firmly but politely, but don't leave it there. Tell them that you're aware of the odds against you. (Something like 20 percent of house sellers attempt to sell their houses without a broker, but only 8 percent succeed. The rest ultimately turn the job over to brokers.) And tell them that you've prepared well for the job. (If you read this book, you will have.)

Also, if you detect that they are reasonable and competent, tell them that you've given yourself a trial period of thirty or sixty days in which to get a sales contract signed, and at that point may be interested in discussing the services of a real estate broker. This may prompt them to be a little more informative, in an effort to impress you as possible future business, and to be more cooperative in talking shop about your house and the market in general.

2
Preparing Your House

You must prepare your house for market because the condition will affect not only its price, but how quickly it sells. A good broker would advise you on how to make your house more marketable. This is something you must do for yourself.

Brokers know that not all houses are ready for the market as soon as you try to sell. Without a good cleaning and some redecorating, many houses remain on the market indefinitely. You may not realize it, but some improvements may be necessary to enable you to receive fair market value for your home.

Put yourself in a buyer's place and consider how a house in poor condition can affect the buyer's price. Look at the property as he or she would. A prospect walking through will figure how much he or she will have to spend on repair and general upgrading.

Since the prospect may be unfamiliar with contractors, local painters, and carpenters, he or she is likely to overestimate the costs involved. An offer will probably be 10 to 20 percent below your asking price, because the prospect will allow that much for upgrading the house.

But, with just 1 to 3 percent of the sale price, you may be able to lay on enough cosmetic improvements that such discounting will never occur. Then you'll stand to recoup the 1 to 3 percent you laid out for the repairs.

WHICH REPAIRS TO MAKE

The key to the repairs is making certain that the result is a bright, clean, and cheerful house that looks and feels well-maintained. First impressions are always the most important when the potential buyer walks through your home. Curb appeal is very important, since prospects are apt to form a definite impression about what they are going to find once they are inside the house. Curb appeal also indicates how well the property has been maintained.

There are no rules of thumb to guide you in what needs doing, but repair work usually consists of cleaning, painting, carpeting, and wallpapering. It may take anywhere from three days to three weeks, depending on the condition of the house. Work usually begins on the exterior of the home.

Consider the following tasks:

- Shampoo carpets and rugs, especially if you have pets.
- Repair cracks on outside and inside walls.
- Paint the interior and exterior.
- Do simple landscaping, such as clearing out weeds and overgrown shrubs and trimming the hedges.
- Remove unsightly wallpaper and carpeting and install new wall covering and flooring.
- Thoroughly clean the interior.

HOW MUCH TO SPEND

There are tables that purport to tell you what a particular upgrading or remodeling job will cost and what the return is likely to be. Usually they are meaningless. There are no average costs, and no house is a typical house. Broadly speaking, however, you won't be compensated for structural repairs, such as foundation repairs, because the buyer expects such items to be in order already. Certain cosmetic repairs can improve your chances of a higher price. Additions that add space can be rewarding. New kitchens and baths usually yield a decent return.

After you assess your house and list needed repairs, solicit bids from several contractors and figure what you'll do yourself. To determine the amount of work that will be done to your house, consider three major factors:

1. *Location*—If your location is desirable, but your house is in poor condition, it may be worth fixing up, since the value of the house probably will increase when the improvements have been completed. On the other hand, if your house is in a poor location and requires extensive and costly work, it may not be worth it. For example, if it lists for $50,000 and costs $10,000 to repair, then it should be worth $60,000. But, if market value of houses in your area only go up to $56,000, the house may not be worth repairing.

2. *Condition*—Before you begin repair work on your house, inspect it carefully for hidden flaws. Once repair work has begun, you are committed to it, and you may find that it is going to be more costly than you thought—perhaps double your estimate. If you don't think the house will support the expense, give the house a good sprucing up and put it on the market at a lower price, billed as a rehabber special, handyman's prize, or remodeler's dream.

3. *Season*—Real estate market activity fluctuates with the time of year. If your house will be on the market in, say, October, when the market naturally slows and finding a buyer becomes more difficult, the repairs may not provide a good return. But, if you put the house on the market in the spring, when market activity turns brisk again and buyers come back into the market, then it could be worth repairing. It may have a better chance of getting a

higher price as a result of the increased market activity.

GENERAL POINTS

One of your major concerns should be getting the work done quickly and on schedule. The longer it takes to prep the house the longer it's off the market. For planning and scheduling purposes, figure that, for the type of cosmetic improvements we're talking about, three to twenty-one days may be necessary for preparation.

Research prices before you decide what needs doing and what doesn't. You want to be as sure as possible that the repairs are necessary and that you will recover your expenditure when the house is sold.

Complete essential repairs before you start with cosmetic improvement. A cathedral ceiling doesn't matter much if the roof leaks.

Acquaint yourself with what buyers are looking for, and don't overimprove. Select improvements for which your market is willing to pay. If your neighborhood won't support a $20,000 kitchen, don't put one in. No matter how hard you try, if your house is worth only $100,000 and you spend $50,000 improving it, you probably won't get $150,000.

Watch your spending. Don't be overcharged on any repairs. Remember, you're going to sell the house, not live in it.

3
The Price of Your House

The crucial step in any transaction is setting the right price. The price can determine how quickly—or slowly—your house will sell. There's no big trick to setting a right price, but without a full grasp of the market, you may set a price that is too high or too low. Figure your price before you put the house on the market. You might even seek legal advice from an attorney.

To set a correct price, you may hire an appraiser, consult with real estate brokers, or do it yourself.

CONSULTING WITH BROKERS

Real estate agents use a variety of statistics and information to present the seller with a "competitive market analysis" to help set a house's asking price. The written form shows recent sales prices and terms of nearby houses, as well as the agent's recommendation of the probable selling price for your home.

The analysis may use a computerized data base that tells Realtors how fast homes are selling and for what percentage of their asking prices.

How do you fox Realtors into setting a price on your house? Ask them to come in and give you their opinion of what it will sell for. Tell them what price will give you the minimum amount of money that *you* expect to walk away with. Then add on their commission. This is the lowest price you should entertain should you hire a broker, and it should be plain to them that if they want to negotiate with the buyer, they will have to set an asking price higher than the one that includes your minimum and their commission. Be prepared for them to want to sign you to a listing contract.

Remember, real estate agents tend to price low. Their main interest is in selling your house as quickly as they can. You may safely assume that you can boost the price a little higher than what the brokers say.

HIRING AN APPRAISER

Some people consider a professional appraisal necessary when you sell your house without a broker. A professional appraisal can be worthwhile if you pick a good appraiser. According to newspaper reports, only about 10 percent of the 150,000 to 200,000 appraisers are members of the half dozen major trade organizations that provide the only educational and performance standards. Many states do not require licensing. Of the handful of states that do license appraisers, most do it by requiring appraisers to have a broker's license. A few states are considering separate licensing, and they are receiving support from the two main trade organizations, the Society of Real Estate Appraisers and the American Institute of Real Estate Appraisers.

Depending on the home's size, the cost will be $100 to $200. Be sure the appraiser uses the Fannie Mae/Freddie Mac appraisal form and is approved by area lenders. In fact, for a word-of-mouth reference at this stage of the process, you may want to call the mortgage loan department at your bank. (For more about appraisals and appraisers, see Chapter 11.)

DO-IT-YOURSELF

If you set the price yourself, you must consider five things:

1. The size and condition of your property
2. Prices of "comparable properties"
3. The availability and type of financing
4. The pace of the market
5. Your motivation to sell

The Concept of Comparable Properties

Evaluate comparable structures in comparable locations. How far afield should you go for comparable properties, and what should you look for when you get to one? Standard practice (and it's certainly not a law) for appraisers calls for them to draw their comparable properties from within a one-mile radius of the subject property. Generally, they like to get as close as they can, even staying on the same block if possible. They don't like to work any harder than anyone else. For many areas the technique is no problem, in the suburbs and subdivisions, for example, where whole neighborhoods are built at the same time, of the same general quality, and within the same price range. With few exceptions, they tend to rise and fall in the same range. Seller motivation and market pressures—the number of houses for sale and the availability of mortgage money—will be major reasons for fluctuations in price.

But, if you've fully rehabbed an old house in an improving city neighborhood, you'll want to extend the search for comparable, fully rehabbed properties within the one-mile radius. This will be your best insurance against setting too low a price.

The Pace of the Market

The pace of the market is determined simply by how fast homes are selling and for what percentage of their asking price. There are two ways to get this information: Monitor brokers' windows and read listings in the classified ads.

And, of course, take up the practice of reading the real estate section of your newspaper. In their articles on the market, reporters usually write about how fast or slow the market is moving. In the heat of a fast-paced market, brokers' windows may be covered with listings that say, "SOLD FIRST DAY, FULL ASKING." Indeed, the authors' own house—which they sold without a broker—was on the market for only five days.

Figuring in the Financing

With regard to financing, your two main concerns are interest rates and availability of money. Terms of financing do affect value. Generally, higher interest rates will suppress prices, and lower interest rates will boost prices—provided sufficient demand is present, of course.

Further, the high interest rates of the early '80s led lenders and developers to create special financing tools to enable buyers to continue to purchase homes at times of high interest rates. Those financing tools affect (usually increase) property value.

In addition, when there's plenty of money for making loans but demand is weak, the appraisal process can be skewed by other factors. The real appraised value becomes less important than making a deal, and that can be a risk for everyone involved.

Pricing Strategy

Based on all these considerations, set a general price range for your house. Then assess your pricing strategy. Generally, there are only two: pricing at the bottom of the range for a quick sale and pricing at the top for maximum profit. Which you choose depends on your motivation to sell. A lower price will make your house easier to buy; a higher price may, if you can wait, put more profit in your pocket. A higher price may also make your house more difficult to sell; if your house does not sell within a few months, you may have to reduce the price.

Remember, you have the sales commission to play with, so even if you give up part of it up front, you're still making no less than you would with a broker. If you price your house a little lower to begin with, you may save yourself some time and ensure a quick and convenient sale. On the other hand, if you think your house will draw top price very quickly, go for it.

Basically, it depends on how much of the sales commission you keep, and how much you give to your buyer.

4
Finding Legal Advice

When you're selling your house without a broker, a good lawyer is your best friend. Having a lawyer who can explain the steps involved in selling and closing a house sale and your rights and responsibilities will save you sleepless nights and perhaps some very expensive mistakes.

Hire an attorney before you place your first advertisement. It probably should be the next thing you do after getting your property spruced up and determining a fair market price.

Because a good lawyer is so crucial to the success of your venture, choosing one should not be taken lightly. Of course, many people who have used a lawyer in the past to draw up a will, settle an insurance claim, or buy their present home may simply turn to the same person for legal advice on their home sale. That lawyer, particularly if you've worked with him or her before on a real estate transaction, may be perfect. But, as Americans become more transient, fewer sellers will have a lawyer they can quickly turn to and whom they know well. Moreover, unless your lawyer handles a great deal of residential real estate, he or she may not be the best one to guide you through this particular legal maze.

PICKING A LAWYER

That's why we recommend that potential sellers seek out a residential real estate specialist, or at least someone who has a fair number of home sales under the belt, someone who is likely to have handled a brokerless transaction before and is comfortable with the process.

You should select a lawyer early because, as rare as it is, your first prospect may turn out to be your buyer, and you don't want to be caught off guard without the legal coaching you need to handle yourself during negotiations and getting the contract signed.

References from business associates and friends who have recently closed a house sale are fertile ground for finding a good attorney. This requires some judgment on your part of course, but if you know someone who is experienced and knowledgeable in real estate matters, his or her legal referral may be all you need.

If you know no lawyers and are starting from ground zero, call your local bar association. Most bar associations will refuse to recommend one or more lawyers by name, even within a specialty like real estate. However, they will confirm the credentials of the lawyer you select. Also, bar associations may know about independent directories drawn up by consumer groups in your area. In large cities, the telephone book usually provides specialist listings for attorneys. Still, if you can turn to trusted friends or relatives for advice on qualified lawyers, you are better off.

Don't stop with just one lawyer's name. Get three or four, in case you don't hit it off with the first lawyer you call. This person is key to the success of your transaction, and while many attorneys are perfectly qualified to handle a simple real estate transaction, not all of them will be easy to work with. You must feel confident that your lawyer is approachable so you will be comfortable asking all kinds of questions.

INTERVIEWING THE ATTORNEYS

Once you put together a list of attorneys, call them and ask each the following questions. Do not be intimidated if some attorneys try to tell you your questions are inappropriate or simplistic. Attorneys are under competitive pressure like never before from the sheer glut of lawyers that were turned out of schools in the '60s and '70s. For once, the law of supply and demand is on your side.

Here are some questions you should include when interviewing the lawyer:

- How many residential real estate transactions have you handled in the past year?
- What percentage of your caseload involves residential and commercial real estate?
- How many *brokerless* residential real estate deals have you handled? How many in the past year?
- Given that I don't have a broker, are you available on short notice, when I get a hot prospect?
- How quickly can you draw up a sales agreement?
- What is your estimated fee for handling a real estate transaction when a seller has a broker?
- What's the fee when the seller does not have a broker?
- Can you refer me to two of your former clients in real estate transactions?

The first three questions tell you how seasoned the attorney is. He or she may not be able to quote the exact number of real estate cases, but attorneys typically keep very good caseload records for their own use and should be able to at least estimate the time they spend representing buyers and sellers. In small towns and suburbs, noncorporate lawyers do a great deal of real estate work along with wills and divorces—it's their bread and butter.

If you find several attorneys who appear experienced in real estate, then your choice will be based on the other points your questions raise: price, philosophy, and client referrals.

Few lawyers will be able to pinpoint their fee. They bill clients by the hour, and no two clients are alike in how much time they will demand. Still, they should be able to give you a fee range with the warning that any unexpected complications could make the meter jump. For a closer comparison, you may want to ask them for their hourly rate. Within a given market, legal fees are likely to be fairly competitive.

Typically, sellers' legal fees will range between $500 and $1,000, depending on your market. Any complications, such as a title challenge or seller financing, will run up your bill from there.

If one attorney's fee seems particularly high or low, ask the client references what they were charged and also ask the attorney to explain the large difference in the fee. If you're on trial for murder, cost may be no object, but most real estate transactions are fairly straightforward, and you may not need (or have to pay for) Melvin Belli to successfully complete the sale of your home.

Finally, when you talk to former clients of each lawyer, ask them to subjectively evaluate their lawyer:

- How long did it take for the lawyer to return phone calls?
- Did he or she refer your paperwork to a paralegal or secretary? (That's not necessarily bad, because it keeps costs down, but if it's a large office and your case is being bounced around, you may get impatient.)
- How well did the lawyer explain the arcane aspects of prorating taxes and insurance?
- How well did the lawyer explain the contract language?

If one of your client referrals turns out to be another for-sale-by-owner, find out how the lawyer worked with the buyer's lawyer. Find out how long it took the lawyer to get the contract hammered out and acceptable to both parties. Was the lawyer available on short notice?

Misunderstandings between you and your buyer can

throw a deal off the track between the time a verbal offer is made and accepted and the sales contract is signed. Your lawyer should be willing to intercede with the buyer's lawyer to straighten things out.

THE LAWYER'S ROLE

Once you've decided on a lawyer, you want a complete rundown of what's ahead, a blow-by-blow account of the sales process from his or her point of view, and a solid understanding of what services are included. Your lawyer should be able to take on the broker's usual role of preparing the seller for the sales process. Tell your lawyer the following:

- You want him or her not only to read the contract, but to represent you in contract negotiations with your buyer's lawyer.
- You want him or her to represent you at closing and to be present at closing.
- You want him or her to handle the paperwork relating to the title and survey.

Here are some questions to ask the lawyer you choose, once you've agreed on the fees and he or she has been hired:

- What's the time line for the project from the time you call for a sales contract to the time money changes hands at closing? What are the bottlenecks? Can the lawyer do anything about them?
- What do you do if they give you earnest money? Does it legally bind you if you accept it? Do you have to take your house off the market? (See Chapter 6.)
- What points of action, inaction, or behavior does the lawyer recommend?
- What documents are needed, so you can get your package together?

You should stay in touch with your attorney as the transaction proceeds. You'll find yourself calling daily for a few days after an offer has been made. When you receive a bona fide offer and your lawyer begins to draw up the sales contract, he or she will ask you for four documents:

1. Title insurance policy
2. Most recent water bill
3. Most recent property tax bill
4. Property survey

In later chapters, we explain what to expect at closing, what your lawyer will provide, and what to expect from the title company.

5
Marketing Your House

How much energy and effort you put into marketing your house depends, more than anything, on whether it is a seller's market or a buyer's market. In a seller's market, where demand is high, mortgage money is plentiful, and interest rates are reasonable; you may have to spend almost no energy, time, or money on marketing. A simple twenty-five-word ad in the local newspaper may be enough to generate a pool of buyers for your house. However, in a buyer's market when demand is sluggish, rates are high, and money tight, you may have to use a full-powered marketing program to create a pool of buyers.

There's one big challenge in either type of market: You have only one house to sell, and it will be competing with hundreds of houses listed for sale by local realty agents. Their multiple-listing service effectively matches prospective buyers with homes meeting their requirements. To compete with the effective multiple-listing service, you must do two things:

1. Precisely and quickly identify your market.
2. Mount a successful marketing campaign.

IDENTIFYING YOUR MARKET

Failing to reach the right market as soon as possible can be the most serious mistake you make. Conventional wisdom has it that your chances of finding a buyer diminish with the length of time the property remains unsold. Depending on the pace of the market, a house may be on the market 1 to 120 days or longer.

Demographics

Demographically, the market for homes divides into:

- Older (retired) people with children grown and gone
- Families, with parent(s) and children
- Couples with no children
- Singles

Common sense tells us certain things about each category.

Older couples likely want single-story (no steps), low-maintenance, smaller homes. They don't want problems. Access to medical care may be important to them.

Families with children will want good schools, sufficient space, safeguards for the children (fences), and most likely will be alert to the quality of the neighborhood.

Couples with no children (so-called empty nesters) may want room to grow or may be looking at their first house as an interim step to a larger home. Maintenance may be less of an item with them than with older couples.

Singles may be most concerned about ease of meeting other singles and about security.

Economics

Consider which demographic group is most likely to be interested in your house. Then qualify them as to economic category:

- Investors
- High-end buyers
- Value seekers
- Rehabbers
- Upwardly mobile

Price of course, determines which economic group you'll be working with.

Investors may be looking for either finished buildings that are easily (and cheaply) maintained or rehab property for quick upgrading and turnaround. They may be looking for no- or low-money-down deals, and they almost certainly will want a positive cash flow on the property. Location may be secondary to them, since they won't be living on the premises.

High-end buyers come in a variety of forms but will focus on either the location, general quality, or both. High-end buyers are the smallest group to draw from and may require the most work to get. They may also be the group to aim for if your house is one of a kind, because the uniqueness will lend distinction to their purchase.

Value seekers can be concerned with energy efficiency, amount of work to be done on the property, and size for the money involved.

Rehabbers are a diverse lot. They may be looking for a house they can pick up for a song, or a house (in the right neighborhood, of course) that people of more modest means wouldn't even consider. The point is, they are always willing to do a lot of work, if the house and the neighborhood have the right *potential*. These people are interested in what the house has that can be worked with. If it has central heat, for example, say so. If it has hardwood floors and lots of Victorian charm, say so. If it has size, say so.

Upwardly mobile types may be looking for a house that requires little to no work, so they don't have to take time away from their careers. They may also be looking for a prestigious address and will give a little on condition to get it.

THE MARKETING CAMPAIGN

Once you determine the primary market for your house, you have to tell these people that your house is for sale and handle the response. This generally means doing at least three things:

1. Writing newspaper ads
2. Answering the phone
3. Showing the home to prospective buyers

Depending on the pace of the market, you may also need to do two more things:

4. Arranging weekend open houses
5. Putting a *For Sale* sign on your front lawn

Writing the Ad

The purpose of the ad is to get people to call you. It should entice but not mislead. Here's what to include:

- Do include asking price. It helps qualify the buyer.
- Don't specifically name the group you're aiming at. It could discourage crossover from other groups.
- Do bring out details of interest to your primary market.
- Don't state "for sale by owner" unless you have a good reason for doing so.
- Describe your property to bring out its best features and those that are unique. The ad is your hook and bait. List the number of bedrooms and number of bathrooms as well as the kind of siding and construction (frame/single). If the basement is finished, say so. If the home is close to schools, transportation, or shopping, say so. Mention any recent remodeling or upgrading. Do you have garage/outbuildings/electric door opener? Special characteristics to mention include private bath off

master bedroom; carpeted throughout; oak floors/ woodwork throughout. State the kind of heating if gas forced air or else something special. Is there central air conditioning or air conditioning at all?
- Mention financing only if you think it is a selling edge or will help qualify your buyer ahead of time.

The following ads include a sample for attracting older couples, plus one for each demographic group.

Sample ad for older couple:

> Maintenance-free 2-bedroom
> brick ranch in beautiful
> condition. Close to hospitals,
> shopping, transportation. Very
> secure home in lovely
> neighborhood. $80,000. Phone
> 555-5555.

Sample ad for investors:

> Clean duplex with both units
> rented. Rents rising in area.
> Positive cash flow at asking
> price. $92,000. Phone 555-5555.

Sample ad for high-end buyers:

> Magnificent 5-bedroom colonial
> with 4 baths, swimming pool, 2
> fireplaces, attached solarium,
> great room. Executive home in
> city's most exclusive area.
> $335,000. Phone 555-5555.

Sample ad for value seekers:

> Energy-efficient 3-bedroom with
> 2,000 sq. ft. of space. Move-in
> condition. Low, low energy bills.
> $80,000. Phone 555-5555.

Sample ad for rehabbers:

> Wonderful old Victorian in up-
> and-coming area. Huge, with all
> the charm waiting to be brought
> out. Oak throughout,
> wainscoting, stained glass—
> more. $80,000. Phone 555-5555.

Sample ad for upwardly mobile:

> Hottest neighborhood in town.
> Fully rehabbed 1920s frame with
> 3 bedrooms, 2 new baths, new
> kitchen, oak throughout, 2-car
> garage, privacy fence, backyard
> deck, full basement/attic, central
> heat/air. $110,000. Phone 555-
> 5555.

Placing the Ad

The ad you've written with the preceding guidelines is generally for newspapers and magazines. What publications you choose and how many you choose depends on your house and market. For example, if your property is a vacation home in a resort area, advertise it in the newspapers of pertinent cities, or you might advertise it in travel magazines. If your house is truly elegant, you may want to include a picture.

Don't spend more than you have to to get the results you want. For example, if your local newspaper is a daily, start the ad in the Sunday edition and every day thereafter for a full week. If a weekly, try your ad for just one week.

Answering the Telephone

If your ad is successful, you will begin to receive telephone calls regarding your property. You may specify in the ad hours at which to call. You may want to buy, rent, or borrow a telephone answering machine or pay for an answering service.

When you do make telephone contact with a prospect, you will follow four steps:

1. "Prequalify" the prospect.
2. Screen the prospect for safety (yours).
3. Entice him or her into seeing your house.
4. Determine the prospect's pertinent selling characteristics.

Prequalifying the Prospect—The price you put in the ad should weed out most of the lookers from the prospects with serious intent, but when the prospect calls, don't be afraid to ask a few questions concerning financial capability. Ask what kind of financing he or she anticipates working with—VHA, FHA, adjustable rate, or whether he or she is seeking owner financing for part or all of the purchase. Ask the prospect what he or she does for a living. If the prospect is a counter helper at a fast-food outlet and your house is listed at $200,000, probe a little deeper. You don't have to be offensive, just interested, so you don't waste your time or theirs.

Screening Prospects—You will also screen prospects to be sure they are not unsavory characters preparing to burglarize your home when you are absent. If the prospect sounds drunk or belligerent, advance cautiously.

Enticing Prospects to Inspect—The biggest and most important job on the telephone, after you've ascertained that you indeed have a hot one on the line, is to entice the prospect into seeing the house, not just driving by. After you've traded preliminary information, press for a definite appointment.

If the prospect resists a definite appointment, ask why. If it's the neighborhood, reassure him or her about it. If it's size of the house, talk about the potential for expansion in your house. Uncover the specific reservations to setting an appointment and overcome them. If the prospect has a specific interest, cater to it. If it's schools, discuss the educational benefits of living in the area.

Defining the Prospect—If, during the course of the conversation, you can get details about the prospect, so much the better. Try some of these questions:

- Are they first-time buyers?
- Do they already own a home and are looking for another to move up to?
- Are they investors?
- Are they looking at the house for themselves or for someone else (elderly parents, for example)?
- If they currently own a house, is it in town or in another state or city (because they've just transferred into yours)?
- Are they living in the house they own?
- Are they moving from a condo into a house?

Each situation will require a little different handling. If the prospects are first-time buyers, remember that they are entering a high-stress situation with the purchase of a house. The investment is sizeable, perhaps the largest they have ever made or ever will make. Try to take the stress out of the experience. Hit the economic benefits of homeownership—mainly the equity and appreciation. Emphasize the luxury of owning a home, the things they can do, the freedom they have to change the property. Make it something they can look forward to.

If they are first-time buyers, find out how long they've been looking, whether your house is the first or tenth house they'll look at. They may not buy your house if it is the first one they look at, or they may make an offer after looking at nine other properties. First-time buyers may bring their parents in for a house tour. That's fine. We encourage it. Get the approval of everyone up front so the rest of the process will go smoothly.

If the prospect is an investor, he or she will want to hear the money side of your pitch. Be prepared to answer questions concerning potential cash flow on the property, state of repair, occupancy or vacancy or vacancy rates, and potential for appreciation.

If a caller is looking for a house for parent or parents, stress the advantages for the elderly.

Lawn Signs

For Sale By Owner signs carry some risk. They can attract the merely curious, which is a real inconvenience. These people are lookers who have no intention to buy. Signs may lead to more problems than opportunities. However, they do promote the fact that your house is for sale.

Open House

If you want to hold an open house, you should post an ad. Also put notices on bulletin boards at work, at the grocery store, wherever the people you want for buyers will see it. Open houses build traffic, so if you are prepared to run one, make the most of it by keeping a visitor's log. Record the names, addresses, and phone numbers of the people who toured your property, so that you can make follow-up calls later on.

Marketing Services

There are services that will help you market your house. Typically these services charge for an advertisement in the service's own publication. The advertisement may carry an ad of forty to fifty words in a single issue for a fee of, say, $60 to $70. An ad that includes a photograph could cost $100. A multiple-issue ad with a phone answering service may run considerably higher. Such services will also make up fact sheets for you and provide *For Sale* signs for your lawn.

Other services, including a rare animal known as a "discount broker," will work for about 1 percent of the sales price, and will provide you with appraisals, attorneys, financing, title insurance, homeowners' insurance, and surveys.

Whether you choose such a service is up to you. You may find them to be more expensive than doing such things yourself. But if time is worth more than money, it may be the way to go.

6
Making the Sale

Unlike a real estate broker, you can't move a hot prospect to your car and on to your office and solicit an offer someplace along the way. Showing your house, soliciting the offer, qualifying your buyer, and negotiating preliminary points of the sales agreement go hand in hand. Showing your house is your big opportunity.

SHOWING YOUR HOUSE

Once you have a definite appointment and have defined the prospect, you can prepare for the encounter. For your personal safety, take these precautions:

- Be sure at least two adults are present when the house is shown to potential buyers.
- If you have expensive baubles, hide them well or put them in your safety deposit box.
- Show to only one prospect at a time.

How you schedule property showings is up to you and your schedule, but allot at least one hour for each tour.

Don't promise anything to your buyer while showing the house, such as guaranteeing the roof is in perfect shape and will never leak. Be upfront and honest about the house's advantages and disadvantages. You don't have to point out its problems, but if the prospect asks directly about an item, answer truthfully. Chances are, if buyers order a professional inspection (and either your buyer or the lender certainly will), they will probably find the problems anyway.

When your prospects arrive, tell them that you're going to give them a quick run-through of the house, just to show them where everything is, and then you're going to turn them loose to go through the house on their own, at their leisure.

During the five-minute tour of the house, point out the details that they might otherwise miss. If you have rewired the kitchen, for example, point out the number of circuits (preferably three). If, when you remodeled the kitchen, you had the foresight to install electric outlets at countertop level, point it out. Countertop outlets are a real convenience. When you run the prospects through the basement, point out that you've expanded the electrical system. If your plumbing system is equipped with clean-outs, point them out as a service convenience. If your windows are special, point them out. You don't have to run on with all the details, but do point out the assets prospects may overlook.

At the end of your five-minute tour, give them a fact sheet similar to the sample that follows. This will contain most of the room dimensions and other pertinent data that they might otherwise feel shy about asking you, or have to pull out a tape measure and get for themselves.

Then, let them go through unattended. It's time to let the house sell itself. Make yourself scarce, but inform them that you will be close by and to please call you if they have any questions. Put yourself at their disposal, but out of their way.

PROPERTY DESCRIPTION/FACT SHEET

Develop a good property description and fill out a fact
sheet that you can hand out to prospective buyers when
they tour the house. The fact sheet on page 36 is modeled
closely on the multiple-listing form used by real estate
brokers. It will help keep the details of your house in the
prospect's mind. Use the Remarks section to call attention
to special features and points of major attraction to your
target market. Also, use the space to list items that stay
with the house, such as custom window coverings or mini-
blinds.

SOLICITING THE OFFER

After a lengthy tour, your prospects will probably know
whether they want to make an offer. The best way for you
to find out is to ask them, "Do you want to make an offer?"

They will say either "Yes," "No," or, "We need some time
to think about it."

There are whole books and schools devoted to teaching
you how best to capitalize on each one of those responses—
how to sell. They teach you about buyer types, selling
techniques, body language, and other esoterica. The body
of knowledge is so extensive that we won't even try to
compete.

At the root of most of it, however, is self-control and
judgment. You can't be emotional about the sale of your
house. Be flexible; adapt your response to the buyer's
attitude and personality. If the prospect's a natural-born
pessimist, give her the positive point of view. If he's a
bargain-hunter and is bent on out-negotiating you, give
him the value side of the argument. If she's a congenial
type, keep it friendly and attentive, and talk about how the
house suits her needs. If he's one of the tough guys—the
argumentative type—pleasantly give the positive side of the
argument and don't get into a fight with him. If he's
analytical, be precise in your response, be patient, and
expect two tours. If the prospect's shy, keep it low-key but

FACT SHEET

No. of rooms: **No. of baths:**   **No. of bedrooms:**
Price:

(Photo, optional, inserted here)

Address: **City:**
Area: **Lot No.:**
Direction/Location: West of (street name)**—South of** (street name),
(3100 N–1800 W)
Incorporated/unincorporated area: Yes   No
Title Insurance: (who with)
Construction: (brick, etc.)   **No. stories:**   **Year built:**
Garage: (no. cars)
Special Assessments: (none known?)
Tax, 19___: (amount for most recent year)
Terms of Possession: (at closing, no. days after closing)
Lot Size: (dimensions in feet)
Living area: (in square feet)
Heat: (what type heat plant)
Appliances: (what stays) ☐ **Range**   ☐ **Refrigerator**
                                   ☐ **Dishwasher**   ☐**Disposal**
Does It Have: ☐ **Porch**   ☐ **Patio**   ☐ **Master Bath**
                            ☐ **Fireplace**   ☐ **Central Air**   ☐ **Wall Air**
Water: ☐ **Well**   ☐ **Private**   ☐ **Municipal**
                ☐ **Water softener:** ☐ **Own**   ☐ **Rent**
Sewer: ☐ **Sanitary**   ☐ **Street**   ☐ **Septic**
Basement: ☐ **Full**   ☐ **¾**   ☐ **½**   ☐ **none**
Transportation: (bus, train, other public transportation serving
location)
Schools: (public/private schools serving area, both elementary
and high school)
Total area (square feet):
Approximate room sizes: (in feet)
   Living Room:
   Dining Room:
   Kitchen:
   Family Room:
   Bedrooms:
   Enclosed Porch(es):
Remarks: (Eat-in kitchen? Garden? Fenced yard? Electric door
opener on garage door? Fully rehabbed? Recent remodeling?
Remind them of the outstanding features they noticed on their
tour. Also, if you have custom window coverings that stay, say
so.)
Owner/Seller: (Your name and telephone number)

be willing to point out benefits that may not be brought up otherwise.

Regardless of how you choose to handle the prospects, if they say "No," find out what their specific objection is to the house. If it's solid, and clearly not just a negotiating ploy, back off, and let them out the door. Ask them to refer the house to any friends who may be interested. If their objection is the price, invite them to make a counteroffer. If their objection is condition of the house, ask what would have to be set right; see if the repairs would be worthwhile (the prospects may be wildly overestimating what they would cost). If the objection is location, you can respond if you have brought yourself up-to-date on the good things happening in your area.

If the response is "We need time to think," try to find out if what they mean is, "Can we afford it?" Offer to sit down and help them figure it out "right now." This book teaches you how to qualify a buyer as a bank would and gives you the forms to do it including charts you can show to your prospect. If affordability isn't the question, ask them how many more houses they have to look at and whether they would like to know when you get a firm offer, just in case they want to make an offer.

Even if you don't get an immediate offer from these people they may call and make an offer later. So, make sure they leave with a fact sheet in hand.

If the response is "Yes," get the price they are willing to pay. If it's low, find out what the reasons are. If they honestly can't afford more than their price, tell them it's too low and let them go. If the price is close, see if they'll go higher—this is the time for some give and take. (Yes, you'll throw in the drapes and washer/dryer, if the buyer can come up on price. Make it easy for them to buy your house.) If they can't come up from the close offer, ask them if you can keep the offer open for a couple of days, to give you time to think about it (and look for better offers). If the offer is right on the button, move on to the next stage.

CONTINGENCIES

Whether your buyers make an offer on the spot or over the phone, you should be alert for certain things. Are your buyers ready to buy now? Or is the purchase contingent on the sale of a house they currently own? If so, the transaction may take some time, depending on how aggressively they sell their house. Is there a co-buyer in the wings who has to see the property before the offer is good? How long do they want to take to find their financing and to close? Is it in line with your schedule?

Such contingencies are not spoilers or necessarily reasons to reject an offer. But they are items to consider that are worth discussing with your lawyer.

QUALIFYING YOUR BUYER

Once you have an offer you like, you should qualify your buyer—make sure the buyer can afford to pay for your house. This important step is described in the next chapter.

NEGOTIATING THE DEAL

By now, you've agreed on the most important aspect to the deal—the price. Beyond a few other minor points (what goes, what stays), don't try to negotiate any farther. Certainly don't try to sign a sales agreement on the spot. This is the time to decide critical aspects of the deal—establish fair fees, negotiate who pays settlement costs, and generally raise questions.

We urge that you let your attorney handle the sales contract and that he or she deal with the buyers' attorney. This keeps you and your buyers from ending up in a personal, and perhaps costly, tug-of-war over details in the agreement. It allows you the distance to maintain your image as a benevolent seller and, therefore, effective salesperson. If things get tough, you can blame it on the lawyers.

To this end, tell your buyers that your lawyer will handle

the contract for you and will get in touch with their lawyer. Ask them who their lawyer is, so you can tell your lawyer.

Let your lawyer know what you want the contract to do for you and for your buyers, as well as any terms you have already committed to orally.

EARNEST MONEY

Until your attorney has received a sales contract, you can keep your property on the market. It may take a few days for the buyers' lawyer or your lawyer to draw up a contract, and in a hot market you may get a better contract offer in that time. Earnest money, though it makes the buyers feel better, does not legally bind the seller to the buyers' offer. To avoid misleading the buyers, many lawyers advise sellers not to ask for earnest money. It's simply up to the buyer—or seller—once an offer has been agreed on to get the contract drawn up as quickly as possible. Ask your lawyer for guidance.

BIDDING UP

If you're selling in a very hot market, you may experience competitive bidding for your house. Your lawyer may become even more valuable by acting as negotiator for you or advising you as you negotiate with the buyers. If you get a better offer before the sales contract has been drawn up and signed, call your lawyer immediately.

7
Qualifying Your Buyer

Though much is made of qualifying your buyer, the proposition is actually fairly simple: Can the prospect afford to buy your house? Can the prospect pass the bank's buyer qualification rules?

The time to qualify your buyer is *after* you have agreed on a firm price and *before* signing a sales agreement, which would remove your property from the market for days, weeks, or months while the buyer seeks financing.

As we mentioned in the previous chapter, you will begin the qualification process on the phone, with a few pertinent questions. Then, when your prospect makes a firm offer and you accept it, you can immediately get into the nitty-gritty of the qualification process. Assure your prospect that all information is strictly confidential and that you're only doing what a good broker would do.

The buyer qualification process focuses on three specific financial points:

1. The buyer's gross monthly income
2. The estimated monthly housing expense

3. The buyer's current total monthly payments on installment debt

Most mortgage lenders figure that the estimated monthly payment should not exceed 28 percent of a borrower's gross monthly income. Some lenders, however, may set the ceiling at 25 percent and others at 30 percent, depending on their individual policy. The total monthly payment and current total monthly liabilities together should not exceed 36 percent of the borrower's gross monthly income. If your buyer doesn't meet these qualifications, his or her chances of qualifying for a mortgage on your house are slim.

The buyer's income-to-debt ratio also may play a role in the qualification process, but it is secondary. As one mortgage loan officer has commented, "I don't care if you owe a million dollars, so long as you only pay out one dollar a month."

TOTAL MONTHLY PAYMENT (PITI)

The total monthly payment or PITI (principal, interest, tax, and insurance) is the basic figure you will use to qualify your buyer. To calculate it, you must know:

- Amount of the down payment
- Interest rate on the mortgage balance after the down payment
- Length of the mortgage
- Approximate real estate tax and hazard (house) insurance the buyer will pay
- Other financing (such as second mortgage)
- Association dues if dwelling is a condominium

Use the sample PITI worksheet on page 42 (excerpted from a loan application) to estimate the monthly payment. Following is a sample calculation based on a conventional thirty-year fixed-rate mortgage.

PITI WORKSHEET

	PRESENT	PROPOSED
Rent	$	
First Mortgage (P&I)		$
Other Financing (P&I)		
Hazard Insurance		
Real Estate Taxes		
Mortgage Insurance		
Homeowner Assn. Dues		
Other:		
Total Monthly Pmt.	$	$
Utilities		
Total	$	$

First, determine mortgage amount:

Selling price	$100,000
less 20 percent down	−20,000
Mortgage amount	$ 80,000

Then determine the approximate monthly payment:

Principal and interest ($80,000 at 10 percent)	$702.40
One-twelfth annual hazard insurance premium (est.)	40.00
One-twelfth annual property tax (est.)	50.00
Total monthly PITI	$792.40

To calculate the monthly principal and interest, use the following amortization tables. Most conventional mortgages are set up for either fifteen or thirty years. To use the tables, find the appropriate interest rate in the left-hand column. Look across to the factor. Multiply the factor by the amount of the mortgage in thousands. In the example, the thirty-year, 10 percent factor of 8.78 was multiplied by $80 (the mortgage amount in thousands) to get a monthly principal and interest payment of $702.40.

Hazard insurance varies with the value of the house, its location, and other factors. It may increase, if the prospects

**15-YEAR PRINCIPAL
AND INTEREST FACTORS**
(8.00% to 15.00%)

Interest Rate	Factor (per $1,000)	Interest Rate	Factor (per $1,000)
8.00%	9.56	11.00	11.37
8.25	9.71	11.25	11.53
8.50	9.85	11.50	11.69
8.75	10.00	11.75	11.85
9.00	10.15	12.00	12.01
9.25	10.30	12.50	12.33
9.50	10.45	13.00	12.66
9.75	10.60	13.50	12.99
10.00	10.75	14.00	13.32
10.25	10.90	14.50	13.66
10.50	11.06	15.00	14.00
10.75	11.21		

**30-YEAR PRINCIPAL
AND INTEREST FACTORS**
(8.00% to 15.00%)

Interest Rate	Factor (per $1,000)	Interest Rate	Factor (per $1,000)
8.00%	7.34	11.00	9.53
8.25	7.52	11.25	9.72
8.50	7.69	11.50	9.91
8.75	7.87	11.75	10.10
9.00	8.05	12.00	10.29
9.25	8.23	12.50	10.68
9.50	8.41	13.00	11.07
9.75	8.60	13.50	11.46
10.00	8.78	14.00	11.85
10.25	8.97	14.50	12.25
10.50	9.15	15.00	12.65
10.75	9.34		

have a fair amount of personal property—art, jewelry, fine furniture—to schedule on the insurance policy. Use the base amount on your current policy, less any fee paid for scheduled property which drives up the cost. If you have doubts, call a local insurance agency (or call two or three) and get a price range on what it will cost to insure only the house and the garage (if the house has one).

For property tax, use the amount you paid last year.

GROSS MONTHLY INCOME

Gross monthly income (income before taxes) is derived from the following:

- Base employment income (job/salary/wages)
- Overtime (if stable and regular)
- Bonuses
- Commissions
- Dividends and interest
- Net rental income
- Other income (child support, alimony, separate maintenance income)

Simply total all the items in this list to arrive at gross monthly income. If the buyer is a two-income family, tally the total for both incomes. You can enter the amounts on the sample income worksheet, which was excerpted from a loan application.

INCOME WORKSHEET

Item	Borrower	Co-Borrower	Total
Base Empl. Income	$	$	$
Overtime			
Bonuses			
Commissions			
Dividends/Interest			
Net Rental Income			
Other			
Total	$	$	$

TOTAL MONTHLY INSTALLMENT PAYMENTS

Monthly installment payments include credit cards, revolving charge accounts, alimony, car loans, child support, and other such installment debt. Use the installment debt worksheet (excerpted from a loan application) to find the total of these payments.

DEBT WORKSHEET

Creditors' Name, Address and Account Number	Acct. Name If Not Borrower's	Mo. Pmt. and Mos. left to pay	Unpaid Balance
Installment Debts (include "revolving" charge accts)		$ Pmt./Mos.	$
		/	
		/	
		/	
		/	
		/	
Other Debts Including Stock Pledges			
		/	
Real Estate Loans		⨯	
Automobile Loans			
		/	
Alimony, Child Support and Separate Maintenance Payments Owed To			⨯
		/	
TOTAL MONTHLY PAYMENTS		$	⨯

WHAT YOUR BUYER CAN AFFORD

The following affordability tables will give you a quick, rough estimate of what your prospects can afford.

THE RESIDENTIAL LOAN APPLICATION

Following the affordability tables is a sample residential loan application. This will give you some idea of the kind of information you'll need. You may want to discuss this with your lawyer.

10%
*Based on a 20% down payment and 30 year-10% mortgage with 25% of your total family income for house payments (principal, interest, taxes and insurance)

1 If your family income is . . .	2 You should be able to handle monthly payments of . . .	3 And you'll need a down payment of about . . .	4 To afford a home costing . . . (Thousands of $)
$14,000	$ 290	$ 6,200	$ 29-32
15,000	310	6,600	32-35
16,000	330	7,000	34-37
17,000	350	7,600	36-40
18,000	375	8,000	38-42
19,000	400	8,400	40-44
20,000	420	8,800	42-46
25,000	520	11,000	53-58
30,000	625	13,200	63-70
35,000	730	15,400	73-81
40,000	830	17,600	84-92
45,000	940	19,800	94-104
50,000	1040	21,800	104-115

12%
*Based on a 20% down payment and 30 year-12% mortgage with 25% of your total family income for house payments (principal, interest, taxes and insurance)

$14,000	$ 290	$ 5,400	$ 26-29
15,000	310	5,800	28-31
16,000	330	6,200	30-33
17,000	350	6,600	32-35
18,000	375	7,000	34-37
19,000	400	7,400	35-39
20,000	420	7,800	37-41
25,000	520	10,000	46-51
30,000	625	12,000	56-62
35,000	730	14,000	65-72
40,000	830	16,200	74-82
45,000	940	18,200	83-92
50,000	1040	20,000	92-102

If you can make a bigger down payment, you can afford a home in the higher ranges below. (Thousands of $)

Column 3 plus $5,000	Column 3 plus $10,000	Column 3 plus $20,000	Column 3 plus $30,000
$ 34-37	$ 37-41	$ 45-49	$ 52-58
36-39	39-44	47-52	54-60
38-42	41-46	49-54	56-62
40-44	44-48	51-56	58-65
42-47	46-51	54-59	60-67
44-49	48-53	55-61	63-69
46-51	50-55	57-63	65-71
57-63	60-67	68-75	75-83
67-74	71-79	78-87	87-95
78-86	81-90	88-97	96-106
88-97	92-101	99-109	106-117
98-109	102-113	110-121	117-130
109-120	112-124	120-133	128-141

Column 3 plus $5,000	Column 3 plus $10,000	Column 3 plus $20,000	Column 3 plus $30,000
$ 30-33	$ 34-37	$ 41-46	$ 49-54
32-35	36-39	43-48	50-56
34-37	38-42	45-50	52-58
36-39	40-44	47-52	54-60
38-41	41-46	49-54	56-62
39-42	43-48	51-56	57-64
41-45	45-50	53-58	59-66
50-56	55-60	62-69	69-76
60-66	64-71	72-79	78-86
69-76	73-81	81-89	87-96
78-86	83-92	91-100	97-107
87-96	92-101	99-110	106-117
95-105	101-112	109-120	115-127

14%

*Based on a 20% down payment and 30 year-14% mortgage with 25% of your total family income for house payments (principal, interest, taxes and insurance)

1 If your family income is . . .	2 You should be able to handle monthly payments of . . .	3 And you'll need a down payment of about . . .	4 To afford a home costing . . . (Thousands of $)
$14,000	$ 290	$ 5,000	$ 23-26
15,000	310	5,400	25-28
16,000	330	5,800	27-30
17,000	350	6,000	28-31
18,000	375	6,400	30-33
19,000	400	6,800	32-35
20,000	420	7,200	33-37
25,000	520	9,000	42-46
30,000	625	10,800	50-55
35,000	730	12,600	58-64
40,000	830	14,400	66-73
45,000	940	16,200	75-83
50,000	1040	18,200	83-92

16%

*Based on a 20% down payment and 30 year-16% mortgage with 25% of your total family income for house payments (principal, interest, taxes and insurance)

$14,000	$ 290	$ 4,400	$ 21-24
15,000	310	4,800	23-25
16,000	330	5,000	24-27
17,000	350	5,400	26-28
18,000	375	5,800	27-30
19,000	400	6,000	29-32
20,000	420	6,400	30-33
25,000	520	8,000	38-42
30,000	625	9,400	45-50
35,000	730	11,000	53-58
40,000	830	12,600	60-66
45,000	940	14,200	68-75
50,000	1040	15,800	75-83

If you can make a bigger down payment, you can afford a home in the higher ranges below. (Thousands of $)

Column 3 plus $5,000	Column 3 plus $10,000	Column 3 plus $20,000	Column 3 plus $30,000
$ 26-29	$ 32-35	$ 40-44	$ 48-53
29-32	33-37	41-46	49-54
31-34	35-38	43-47	51-56
32-36	36-40	45-49	53-58
34-38	38-42	46-51	54-60
36-40	40-44	48-53	56-62
38-42	41-46	50-55	58-64
46-51	50-55	58-64	66-73
54-60	58-64	66-73	74-82
63-69	66-73	75-83	82-91
71-79	75-82	83-91	91-100
79-88	83-92	99-101	99-110
88-97	91-101	100-110	107-119

Column 3 plus $5,000	Column 3 plus $10,000	Column 3 plus $20,000	Column 3 plus $30,000
$ 25-28	$ 29-32	$ 38-41	$ 45-50
27-30	31-34	39-43	47-52
28-31	32-36	40-45	48-53
30-33	34-37	42-46	50-55
31-35	35-39	43-48	52-57
33-36	37-41	45-50	53-59
34-38	38-42	46-51	55-60
42-46	46-51	54-60	62-68
49-54	53-59	61-68	69-77
56-62	61-67	69-76	77-85
64-70	68-75	76-84	84-93
72-79	76-84	84-92	92-101
79-87	83-92	91-101	99-110

RESIDENTIAL LOAN APPLICATION

| MORTGAGE APPLIED FOR | ☐ Conventional ☐ FHA ☐ VA | Amount $ | Interest Rate % | No. of Months | Monthly Payment Principal & Interest | Escrow/Impounds (to be collected monthly) ☐ Taxes ☐ Hazard Ins. ☐ Mtg. Ins. |

Prepayment Option

| Property Street Address | | City | County | State | Zip | No. Units |

Legal Description (Attach description if necessary)

Year Built

| Purpose of Loan: ☐ Purchase ☐ Construction-Permanent ☐ Construction ☐ Refinance ☐ Other (Explain) |

| Complete this line if Construction-Permanent or Construction Loan | Lot Value Data | | | | |
| | Year Acquired | Original Cost $ | Present Value (a) $ | Cost of Imps. (b) $ | Total (a + b) $ |

ENTER TOTAL AS PURCHASE PRICE IN DETAILS OF PURCHASE.

| Complete this line if a Refinance Loan | | | | | |
| Year Acquired | Original Cost $ | Amt. Existing Liens $ | Purpose of Refinance | Describe Improvements [ ] made [ ] to be made |

Cost: $

Title Will Be Held In What Name(s)

Manner In Which Title Will Be Held

Source of Down Payment and Settlement Charges

This application is designed to be completed by the borrower(s) with the lender's assistance. The Co-Borrower Section and all other Co-Borrower questions must be completed and the appropriate box(es) checked if ☐ another person will be jointly obligated with the Borrower on the loan, or ☐ the Borrower is relying on income from alimony, child support or separate maintenance or on the income or assets of another person as a basis for repayment of the loan, or ☐ the Borrower is married and resides, or the property is located, in a community property state.

BORROWER				CO-BORROWER			
Name		Age	School Yrs	Name		Age	School Yrs
Present Address	No. Years ___ ☐ Own ☐ Rent			Present Address	No. Years ___ ☐ Own ☐ Rent		
Street				Street			
City/State/Zip				City/State/Zip			
Former address if less than 2 years at present address				Former address if less than 2 years at present address			
Street				Street			
City/State/Zip				City/State/Zip			
Years at former address		☐ Own ☐ Rent		Years at former address		☐ Own ☐ Rent	
Marital Status ☐ Married ☐ Separated ☐ Unmarried (incl. single, divorced, widowed)	DEPENDENTS OTHER THAN LISTED BY CO-BORROWER NO. AGES			Marital Status ☐ Married ☐ Separated ☐ Unmarried (incl. single, divorced, widowed)	DEPENDENTS OTHER THAN LISTED BY BORROWER NO. AGES		
Name and Address of Employer		Years employed in this line of work or profession?		Name and Address of Employer		Years employed in this line of work or profession?	

SUBJECT PROPERTY

Lending institutions will use this form to qualify and approve your buyer's loan.

			Years on this job _____ years □ Self Employed*					Years on this job _____ years □ Self Employed*
Position/Title		Type of Business		**Position/Title**			Type of Business	
Social Security Number*	Home Phone		Business Phone	**Social Security Number***	Home Phone			Business Phone

GROSS MONTHLY INCOME

Item	Borrower	Co-Borrower	Total
Base Empl. Income	$	$	$
Overtime			
Bonuses			
Commissions			
Dividends/Interest			
Net Rental Income			
Other† (Before completing, see notice under Describe Other Income below.)			
Total	$	$	$

MONTHLY HOUSING EXPENSE **

	PRESENT	PROPOSED
Rent	$	
First Mortgage (P&I)		$
Other Financing (P&I)		
Hazard Insurance		
Real Estate Taxes		
Mortgage Insurance		
Homeowner Assn. Dues		
Other:		
Total Monthly Pmt.	$	$
Utilities		
Total	$	$

DETAILS OF PURCHASE
Do Not Complete If Refinance

a. Purchase Price	$
b. Total Closing Costs (Est.)	
c. Prepaid Escrows (Est.)	
d. Total (a + b + c)	$
e. Amount This Mortgage	( )
f. Other Financing	( )
g. Other Equity	( )
h. Amount of Cash Deposit	( )
i. Closing Costs Paid by Seller	( )
j. Cash Reqd. For Closing (Est.)	$

DESCRIBE OTHER INCOME

B—Borrower   C—Co-Borrower

NOTICE:† Alimony, child support, or separate maintenance income need not be revealed if the Borrower or Co-Borrower does not choose to have it considered as a basis for repaying this loan.

	Monthly Amount
	$

IF EMPLOYED IN CURRENT POSITION FOR LESS THAN TWO YEARS COMPLETE THE FOLLOWING

B/C	Previous Employer/School	City/State	Type of Business	Position/Title	Dates From/To	Monthly Income
						$

THESE QUESTIONS APPLY TO BOTH BORROWER AND CO BORROWER

	Borrower Yes or No	Co-Borrower Yes or No	If applicable, explain Other Financing or Other Equity (provide addendum if more space is needed).
If a "yes" answer is given to a question in this column, explain on an attached sheet.			
Have you any outstanding judgments? In the last 7 years, have you been declared bankrupt?			
Have you had property foreclosed upon or given title or deed in lieu thereof?			
Are you a co-maker or endorser on a note?			
Are you a party in a law suit?			
Are you obligated to pay alimony, child support, or separate maintenance?			
Is any part of the down payment borrowed?			

This Statement and any applicable supporting schedules may be completed jointly by both married and unmarried co-borrowers if their assets and liabilities are sufficiently joined so that the Statement can be meaningfully and fairly presented on a combined basis; otherwise separate Statements and Schedules are required (FHLMC 65A/FNMA 1003A). If the co-borrower section was completed about a spouse, this statement and supporting schedules must be completed about that spouse also. ☐ Completed Jointly ☐ Not Completed Jointly

STATEMENT OF ASSETS AND LIABILITIES

ASSETS		LIABILITIES AND PLEDGED ASSETS			
		Indicate by (*) those liabilities or pledged assets which will be satisfied upon sale of real estate owned or upon refinancing of subject property			
Description	Cash or Market Value	Creditors' Name, Address and Account Number	Acct. Name if Not Borrower's	Mo. Pmt. and Mos. left to pay	Unpaid Balance
Cash Deposit Toward Purchase Held By	$	Installment Debts (include "revolving" charge accts)		$ Pmt./Mos.	$
Checking and Savings Accounts (Show Names of Institutions/Acct. Nos.)				/	
				/	
Stocks and Bonds (No./Description)				/	
				/	
Life Insurance Net Cash Value Face Amount ($ ___)		Other Debts Including Stock Pledges		/	
SUBTOTAL LIQUID ASSETS	$			/	
Real Estate Owned (Enter Market Value from Schedule of Real Estate Owned)		Real Estate Loans		/	
Vested Interest in Retirement Fund					
Net Worth of Business Owned (ATTACH FINANCIAL STATEMENT)					
Automobiles (Make and Year)		Automobile Loans		/	
Furniture and Personal Property		Alimony, Child Support and Separate Maintenance Payments Owed To		/	
Other Assets (Itemize)					
		TOTAL MONTHLY PAYMENTS		$	
TOTAL ASSETS	A $	NET WORTH (A minus B) $		TOTAL LIABILITIES	B $

SCHEDULE OF REAL ESTATE OWNED (If Additional Properties Owned Attach Separate Schedule)

Address of Property (Indicate S if Sold, PS if Pending Sale or R if Rental being held for income)	◇	Type of Property	Present Market Value	Amount of Mortgages & Liens	Gross Rental Income	Mortgage Payments	Taxes, Ins. Maintenance and Misc.	Net Rental Income
			$	$	$	$	$	$
		TOTALS ➞	$	$	$	$	$	$

LIST PREVIOUS CREDIT REFERENCES

◇	B – Borrower C – Co-Borrower	Creditor's Name and Address	Account Number	Purpose	Highest Balance	Date Paid
					$	

List any additional names under which credit has previously been received _____

AGREEMENT: The undersigned applies for the loan indicated in this application to be secured by a first mortgage or deed of trust on the property described herein, and represents that the property will not be used for any illegal or restricted purpose, and that all statements made in this application are true and are made for the purpose of obtaining the loan. Verification may be obtained from any source named in this application. The original or a copy of this application will be retained by the lender, even if the loan is not granted. The undersigned ☐ intend or ☐ do not intend to occupy the property as their primary residence.

I/we fully understand that it is a federal crime punishable by fine or imprisonment, or both, to knowingly make any false statements concerning any of the above facts as applicable under the provisions of Title 18, United States Code, Section 1014.

Borrower's Signature _____ Date _____ Co-Borrower's Signature _____ Date _____

INFORMATION FOR GOVERNMENT MONITORING PURPOSES

The following information is requested by the Federal Government if this loan is related to a dwelling, in order to monitor the lender's compliance with equal credit opportunity and fair housing laws. You are not required to furnish this information, but are encouraged to do so. The law provides that a lender may neither discriminate on the basis of this information, nor on whether you choose to furnish it. However, if you choose not to furnish it, under Federal regulations this lender is required to note race and sex on the basis of visual observation or surname. If you do not wish to furnish the above information, please initial below

BORROWER: I do not wish to furnish this information (initials) _____

RACE/ NATIONAL ORIGIN ☐ American Indian, Alaskan Native ☐ Asian, Pacific Islander ☐ Black ☐ Hispanic ☐ White ☐ Other (specify) _____

SEX: ☐ Female ☐ Male

CO-BORROWER: I do not wish to furnish this information (initials) _____

RACE/ NATIONAL ORIGIN ☐ American Indian, Alaskan Native ☐ Asian, Pacific Islander ☐ Black ☐ Hispanic ☐ White ☐ Other (specify) _____

SEX ☐ Female ☐ Male

FOR LENDER'S USE ONLY

(FNMA REQUIREMENT ONLY) This application was taken by ☐ face to face interview ☐ by mail ☐ by telephone

_____ (Interviewer)   Name of Employer of Interviewer _____

8
The Sales Agreement

A broker's basic objective is to obtain a signed contract of sale that properly expresses the agreement between you and your buyer. Take this as your basic goal, too.

Speed is important at this time. You don't want to give people time to back out or change their minds before they sign. If you strike an oral deal in the morning, get your lawyer working on it the same afternoon. If you agree in the evening, the next morning should be your target time. You want the contract completed and signed within a few days.

Bear in mind that there is no standard contract that you are required to sign. You are entitled to make any modifications in or additions to any standard form contract to which the buyer will agree. But the sales agreement you and the buyer sign is generally the deal you live with; subsequent changes may be difficult to negotiate. So, make sure the contract does what you want it to do.

While reading the following description of typical contract terms, refer to the sample contract on pages 56–59.

GENERAL CONTRACT ITEMS

The contract includes several general items, which form the base of the contract, and specify price, financing, and time limits:

1. The signed agreement should state exactly which settlement costs you will pay and which will be paid by your buyer. (See Chapter 12 for more information about these costs.)
2. Usually, the nut of the agreement is that you, the seller, provide title, free and clear of all liens and encumbrances except those which you specify in the contract or approve when the results of the title search are reported to you.
3. The contract should specify that some amount of earnest money be held in escrow for the deal. How much is up to you, the buyer, and the attorneys. If the deal should fall through, the earnest money may go to you or revert to your buyer, depending on how it is set up. The earnest money commonly is held by a joint guaranteed account with interest to the buyer.
4. The contract also should specify the amount of time the buyer has to find financing for a specific amount at a specific interest rate (usually worded "with interest not to exceed"), and the duration of the loan (fifteen or thirty years, usually).
5. The date of closing will be stated, for example "September 5, 1986," as will the place of closing, which may be the office of your lawyer or the buyer's, or the lending institution.
6. The contract should indicate when the buyer will take possession—any time from the same day as closing to thirty, sixty, ninety days or more after closing. This is something to work out with your buyer.
7. Usually the contract specifies how much you agree to pay your broker in sales commissions. But, since

Real Estate Sale Contract

1. _____ (Purchaser)

agrees to purchase at a price of $ _____ on the terms set forth herein, the following described real estate

in _____ County, Illinois: _____ is

(If legal description is not included at time of execution,
authorized to insert thereafter.)

commonly known as _____ , and

with approximate lot dimensions of _____ x _____ , together with the following personal property presently located thereon:
(strike items not applicable) (a) storm and screen doors and windows; (b) awnings; (c) outdoor television antenna; (d) wall-to-wall, hallway and stair
carpeting; (e) window shades and draperies and supporting fixtures; (f) venetian blinds; (g) electric, plumbing and other attached fixtures as installed;
(h) water softener; (i) refrigerator(s); (j) _____ range(s); (k) garage door opener with _____ transmitters; (l) radiator
covers; (m) indoor and outdoor (louvered) shutters; and also

2. _____ (Seller)

(Insert names of all owners and their respective spouses)

agrees to sell the real estate and the property, if any, described above at the price and terms set forth herein, and to convey or cause to be conveyed to
Purchaser or nominee title thereto (in joint tenancy) by a recordable _____ deed, with release of homestead rights, and a proper bill
of sale, subject only to: (a) covenants, conditions and restrictions of record; (b) private, public and utility easements and roads and highways, if any; (c)
party wall rights and agreement, if any; (d) existing leases and tenancies; (e) special taxes or assessments for improvements not yet completed; (f) any
unconfirmed special tax or assessment; (g) installments not due at the date hereof of any special tax or assessment for improvements heretofore
completed; (h) mortgage or trust deed specified below, if any; (i) general taxes for the year _____ and subsequent years including taxes which may
accrue by reason of new or additional improvements during the year(s) _____ ; and to

3. Purchaser has paid $ _____ (and will pay within _____ days the additional sum of $ _____) as earnest money to be
applied on the purchase price, and agrees to pay or satisfy the balance of the purchase price, plus or minus prorations, at the time of closing as follows: :
(strike subparagraph not applicable)

(a) The payment of $ _____

(b) The acceptance of the title to the real estate by Purchaser subject to a mortgage (trust deed) of record securing a principal indebtedness (which the
Purchaser [does] [does not] agree to assume) aggregating $ _____ bearing interest at the rate of _____ % a year, and the
payment of a sum which represents the difference between the amount due on the indebtedness at the time of closing and the balance of the
purchase price.

...............or sell to procure within _____ days a firm commitment for a loan to be secured by a mortgage or trust deed on the real estate in the amount of $ _____ , or such lesser sum as Purchaser accepts, with interest not to exceed _____ % a year to be amortized over _____ years, the commission and service charges for such loan not to exceed _____ %. If, after making every reasonable effort, Purchaser is unable to procure such commitment within the time specified herein and so notified Seller thereof within that time, this contract shall become null and void and all earnest money shall be returned to Purchaser; provided that if Seller, at his option, within a like period of time following Purchaser's notice, procures for Purchaser such a commitment or notifies Purchaser that Seller will accept a purchase money mortgage upon the same terms, this contract shall remain in full force and effect. *(Strike paragraph if inapplicable.)*

5. The time of closing shall be on _____ , or 20 days after notice that financing has been procured if above paragraph 4 is operative, or on the date, if any, to which such time is extended by reason of paragraph 2 of the Conditions and Stipulations hereafter becoming operative (whichever date is later), unless subsequently mutually agreed otherwise, at the office of _____ or of the mortgage lender, if any, provided title is shown to be good or is accepted by Purchaser.

6. Seller shall deliver possession to Purchaser on or before _____ days after the sale has been closed. Seller agrees to pay Purchaser the sum of $ _____ for each day Seller remains in possession between the time of closing and the time possession is delivered.

7. Seller agrees to pay a broker's commission to _____ in the amount set forth in the broker's listing contract or as follows: _____

8. The earnest money shall be held by _____ for the mutual benefit of the parties.

9. Seller agrees to deliver possession of the real estate in the same condition as it is at the date of this contract, ordinary wear and tear excepted.

10. A duplicate original of this contract, duly executed by the Seller and his spouse, if any, shall be delivered to the Purchasers within _____ days from the date below, otherwise, at the Purchaser's option, this contract shall become null and void and the earnest money shall be refunded to the Purchaser.

This contract is subject to the Conditions and Stipulations set forth on the back page hereof, which Conditions and Stipulations are made a part of this contract.

Dated _____

Purchaser _____   (Address) _____

Purchaser _____   (Address) _____

Seller _____   (Address) _____

Seller _____   (Address) _____

*Form normally used for sale of residential property of four or fewer units.

CONDITIONS AND STIPULATIONS

1. Seller shall deliver or cause to be delivered to Purchaser or Purchaser's agent, not less than 5 days prior to the time of closing, a title commitment for an owner's title insurance policy issued by the Chicago Title Insurance Company in the amount of the purchase price, covering title to the real estate on or after the date hereof, showing title in the intended grantor subject only to (a) the general exceptions contained in the policy unless the real estate is improved with a single family dwelling or an apartment building of four or fewer residential units, (b) the title exceptions set forth above, and (c) title exceptions pertaining to liens or encumbrances of a definite or ascertainable amount which may be removed by the payment of money at the time of closing and which the Seller may so remove at that time by using the funds to be paid upon the delivery of the deed (all of which are herein referred to as the permitted exceptions). The title commitment shall be conclusive evidence of good title as therein shown as to all matters insured by the policy, subject only to the exceptions as therein stated. Seller also shall furnish Purchaser an affidavit of title in customary form covering the date of closing and showing title in Seller subject only to the permitted exceptions in foregoing items (b) and (c) and unpermitted exceptions, if any, as to which the title insurer commits to extend insurance in the manner specified in paragraph 2 below.

2. If the title commitment discloses unpermitted exceptions, Seller shall have 30 days from the date of delivery thereof to have the exceptions removed from the commitment or to have the title insurer commit to insure against loss or damage that may be occasioned by such exceptions, and, in such event, the time of closing shall be 35 days after delivery of the commitment or the time specified in paragraph 5 on the front page hereof, whichever is later. If Seller fails to have the exceptions removed, or in the alternative, to obtain the commitment for title insurance specified above as to such exceptions within the specified time, Purchaser may terminate this contract or may elect, upon notice to Seller within 10 days after the expiration of the 30-day period, to take title as it then is with the right to deduct from the purchase price liens or encumbrances of a definite or ascertainable amount. If Purchaser does not so elect, this contract shall become null and void without further actions of the parties.

3. Rents, premiums under assignable insurance policies, water and other utility charges, fuels, prepaid service contracts, general taxes, accrued interest on mortgage indebtedness, if any, and other similar items shall be adjusted ratably as of the time of closing. If the amount of the current general taxes is not then ascertainable, the adjustment thereof shall be on the basis of the amount of the most recent ascertainable taxes. The amount of any general taxes which may accrue by reason of new or additional improvements shall be adjusted as follows: _____

All prorations are final unless otherwise provided herein. Existing leases and assignable insurance policies, if any, shall then be assigned to Purchaser. Seller shall pay the amount of any stamp tax imposed by State law on the transfer of the title, and shall furnish a completed Real Estate Transfer Declaration signed by the Seller or the Seller's agent in the form required pursuant to the Real Estate Transfer Tax Act of the State of Illinois and shall furnish any declaration signed by the Seller or the Seller's agent or meet other requirements as established by any local ordinance with regard to a transfer or transaction tax; such tax required by local ordinance shall be paid by the party upon whom such ordinance places responsibility therefor. If such transaction tax; such tax shall be paid by the (Purchaser) (Seller). *(strike one.)*

4. The provisions of the Uniform Vendor and Purchaser Risk Act of the State of Illinois shall be applicable to this contract.

5. If this contract is terminated without Purchaser's fault, the earnest money shall be returned to the Purchaser, but if the termination is caused by the Purchaser's fault, then at the option of the Seller and upon notice to the Purchaser, the earnest money shall be forfeited to the Seller and applied first to the payment of Seller's expenses and then to payment of broker's commission; the balance, if any, to be retained by the Seller as liquidated damages.

6. At the election of Seller or Purchaser upon notice to the other party not less than 5 days prior to the time of closing, this sale shall be closed through an escrow with Chicago Title and Trust Company, in accordance with the general provisions of the usual form of Deed and Money Escrow Agreement then in use by Chicago Title and Trust Company, with such special provisions inserted in the escrow agreement as may be required to conform with this contract. Upon the creation of such an escrow, anything herein to the contrary notwithstanding, payment of purchase price and delivery of deed shall be made through the escrow and this contract and the earnest money shall be deposited in the escrow. The cost of the escrow shall be divided equally between Seller and Purchaser. *(Strike paragraph if inapplicable.)*

7. Time is of the essence of this contract.

8. All notices herein required shall be in writing and shall be served on the parties at the addresses following their signatures. The mailing of a notice by registered or certified mail, return receipt requested, shall be sufficient service.

9. Purchaser and Seller hereby agree to make all disclosures and do all things necessary to comply with the applicable provisions of the Real Estate Settlement Procedures Act of 1974. In the event that either party shall fail to make appropriate disclosure when asked, such failure shall be considered a breach on the part of said party.

FORM 3772 R. 3/79

you haven't employed a broker, state, "The parties warrant that neither have engaged the services of a real estate agent or broker."

8. The contract will usually commit you to deliver the house in the same condition as it is at the date of the contract, with ordinary wear and tear excepted.

9. Another possible provision limits the amount of time you have to deliver a signed duplicate of the contract to your buyer—maybe seven days from the date it is signed. If you don't deliver it by then, the buyer has the right to claim the contract null and void.

CONDITIONS AND STIPULATIONS

The general contract items are subject to certain conditions and stipulations included in the contract. These conditions and stipulations may include the following:

1. You give the buyer clear title and a title commitment for owner's title insurance at some time before closing.

2. You agree to remove, within certain time limits, any liens or encumbrances against the title to your property, or else your buyer may cancel the contract.

3. Property taxes and similar items shall be prorated at closing. That is, you'll pay the taxes while you're in the house, and your buyer will pay taxes from the moment he or she assumes title to the property.

4. Certain state laws shall govern the contract.

5. The earnest money may revert to either you or your buyer, depending on the reason the contract is terminated.

6. Either you or your buyer may opt to close the deal through an escrow account with proper notification to the other side.

7. Time is of the essence of the contract. Basically, this means that neither you nor your buyer

should engage in unnecessary delay tactics in meeting the times set forth in the contract. If unnecessary delays hurt either financially (and such damage must be proved), the contract could be voided, or damages could be awarded, or both.

8. All notices and communications affecting the contract must be in writing.

9. You and your buyer are being honest. If either party is dishonest in words or actions, that party will be in breach of contract.

10. By a specific date, you will provide a recent survey of the property acceptable to your buyer's lender.

11. You agree to pay a daily rent of X dollars if you have to stay in the house past the date of possession agreed upon in the basic contract.

AMENDMENTS AND RIDERS

Your buyer's lawyer will no doubt attach an amendment, or rider, to the basic contract your lawyer draws up. It will contain provisions that your buyer wants included in the contract and, usually, will state that if there is a conflict between the provisions of the contract and the amendment, the provisions of the amendment will have priority. The amendment will include any special points that you discussed with your buyer when you struck the deal, and may include other points that the buyer's lawyer wants to include. In addition to reading the following list of amendment points, refer to the sample rider on pages 62–63.

Usually, the sequence for this is as follows: Your lawyer draws up the basic contract, then sends it to the buyer's lawyer. The buyer's lawyer will attach the amendment and send the package back to your lawyer. At this time, your lawyer should call you, explain the meaning of the provisions in the amendment and recommend any changes that might be to your advantage.

A special note: Your buyer's lawyer will want you to "warrant," that is, guarantee, certain things about the house. Your lawyer should guard against any such guarantees, so far as is reasonable.

RIDER ATTACHED TO AND MADE A PART OF THE REAL ESTATE SALE CONTRACT MADE BY AND
BETWEEN   (PURCHASER) AND
(SELLER), RELATIVE TO THE PROPERTY COMMONLY KNOWN AS

This Rider is incorporated in and made a part of the Real Estate Sales
Contract to which it is attached. In the event of a conflict between this
Rider and the Real Estate Sales Contract, this Rider shall control.

BUILDING
VIOLATIONS

Seller represents that Seller has received no
notice of building, health, fire or other code
violations affecting the unit or the common
elements.

CONDITION OF
APPLIANCES AND
SYSTEMS

Seller represents that all appliances and all
electric, plumbing, heating systems within the
unit shall be in working condition at closing.

CONDOMINIUM
ASSESSMENT
AND TAXES

Seller represents that the monthly assessment on the
unit as of _____, is approximately
$_____, that no special or extraordinary
assessments are expected or contemplated, and that
the annual real estate taxes on the unit as of
_____ (for the year _____) are
approximately $_____.

EXPIRATION
OF LOAN
COMMITMENT

It is expressly understood and agreed that
Purchaser's mortgage loan commitment, if any,
will, under usual and customary institutional
lending practices, expire within 60 to 90 days
after the date of issuance. In the event
closing does not occur within such 60 to 90
days, or by the date, if later, on which
Purchaser's mortgage loan commitment actually
expires, then Purchaser may, at Purchaser's
election, terminate this contract by giving
written notice to Seller, and this contract
shall become null and void and all earnest
money shall be returned to Purchaser.

INSPECTION

This contract is subject to the condition that an
engineer employed by Purchaser inspect the
improvements, including, but not limited to, the
unit and the common elements, within ten (10) days
of Seller's acceptance of this contract. If the
report thereon of such engineer is not reasonably
satisfactory according to the standards generally
accepted by qualified engineers, to the Purchaser
and notice of such unsatisfactory report is given
to the Seller or Seller's attorney within two (2)
days thereafter, then the contract is null and void
and the earnest money shall be returned to Purchaser.
In addition, Purchaser shall have the right to inspect the unit twice during the ten (10) days
preceding the closing.

CLOSING Seller shall furnish to Purchaser's attorney, not less than three (3) days prior to closing, unexecuted copies of all documents to be delivered to Purchaser at closing.

SURVEY Seller shall provide at closing a Survey of the unit, the building, and all common elements, showing no encroachments.

STORAGE AND GARAGE SPACE Seller warrants that Seller has the right or title to at least one storage locker and one parking space, which shall be assigned to Purchaser at closing, in the same manner as in the conveyance of title as provided herein.

PRORATION OF REAL ESTATE TAXES The parties agree to prorate the accrued real estate taxes on the basis of 110% of the _____ taxes, as determined by the _____ final bill.

ADDITIONAL DOCUMENTS Seller shall provide the following items to Purchaser's attorney within five (5) days of acceptance of this contract:

1. Copy of existing title policy.

2. Copy of existing survey.

3. Copy of building hazard insurance policy.

4. Copy of Declaration of Condominium Ownership, By-Laws, Rules and Regulations.

5. Copy of 19___ - 19___ operating budget.

6. Engineering report, if it exists.

This Contract is subject to approval of such documents by Purchaser's attorney, which documents, if not disapproved within five (5) days from receipt of same, shall be deemed approved.

PURCHASER: SELLER:

_____   _____

_____   _____

Some points that may be in the amendment include the following:

1. You, the seller, don't know of any code violations on the property, and if any come up before closing, you'll notify the buyer immediately—and cure the violation.
2. The contract is contingent upon a professional house inspection, paid for by the buyer. Usually, the inspection must be performed within a specific time of the signing of the sales contract.
3. You will remove debris, and trash, from the property; essentially, you will leave the property clean and in good shape.
4. You represent—but do not warrant—that the heating, cooling, plumbing, and electrical systems are in good operating condition and will be so when the buyer takes possession.
5. Interest on the earnest money will go to your buyer whether or not the deal goes through.
6. Except for the specific provisions of the amendment, all other terms and conditions of the contract are confirmed.

Again, there is no standard contract. The examples in this chapter are just that, examples. If you want specific conditions included in the contract, tell your lawyer. If you object to specific conditions proposed by your buyer, tell your lawyer. With a little patience, most disagreements can be worked out to mutual satisfaction.

9
Helping Find the Financing

Normally, a good listing broker will shag financing for the buyer. It's important that you provide the same service.

Helping the buyer find financing makes it easier for the buyer to purchase your property, speeds the deal along, and gives the lawyer confidence in you as a seller, which keeps the deal smooth. At the least, inform your buyers that you are happy to provide the help. If they say "No" and seem capable of handling it themselves, fine, just let them know you're on hand if they need you. If they say they would like the assistance, drive on.

In working with the lenders, your goal is to help your buyer secure financing—a mortgage commitment—as soon as possible.

Consider first which type of financing your buyer is seeking:

- Conventional mortgage with a full 20 percent down
- An insured conventional mortgage with 10 percent down
- VA/FHA mortgage

- Assumption of your mortgage
- Financing from you

CONVENTIONAL MORTGAGES

Fifteen- and thirty-year conventional mortgages, some of which are insured, account for the bulk of all mortgages. So, a conventional loan probably is the type your buyer seeks. Banks, savings and loan associations (S&Ls), and mortgage bankers offer conventional mortgages.

When you call them for information, ask for the following:

- Interest rates
- Whether they will lock in the rate
- Discount points
- Origination fee
- Application fee
- Lawyer's fee

Compare the interest rates at a half-dozen or more banks. Whether you do it by reading the newspaper or calling the institutions themselves, it won't take more than fifteen to twenty minutes. Nowadays, a mortgage rate table is a common feature in newspapers. Pick the banks with the lowest rates, so that your buyers will know you're operating in their best interests.

In general, S&Ls offer locks on their rates; mortgage bankers do not. This means that S&Ls will lock in the loan at the rate that is current when they approve the loan. This is important if there is a long lag time between approving the loan and closing the sale. With no lock on the rate, the interest rate could rise, causing your buyer to back out of the deal and leave you stuck. To protect yourself, try to help your buyer get a loan with a locked interest rate.

Lending institutions commonly offer a range of interest rates with different discount points to pay. An institution may, for example, offer rates from 9.75 percent to 10.5 percent. A borrower who wants the lowest rate will have to pay money—points—up front to get it. At 9.75 percent, the points may be 4.9 percent of the total mortgage balance sought. The points will decrease as the interest rate rises, perhaps reaching zero at the highest rate, in this example, 10.5 percent.

Lenders may charge for "originating" the loan, with fees ranging from 2 percent to 3 percent of the loan amount down to nothing. Whatever the amount, figure it into the buyer's total financing package. The fee covers the lender's administrative cost in processing the loan. Generally, the buyer pays the fee unless another arrangement has been made with the seller and written into the sales contract.

Some lenders charge a nonrefundable loan application fee; others don't. Fees will vary. A representative range would be $150 to $250.

A lender may charge for legal services needed in connection with the settlement, such as examination of the title binder or sales contract. Fees can range up to $300. Normally, they are paid by the buyer.

After you have a good sampling of institutions, pick the ones that have the lowest rates, lock in rates, and have decent discount fees. Call these banks back, and when you talk to mortgage loan officers, explain that you're a FSBO and ask whether they would be willing to do you a favor by setting up an early appointment. Remember, you are throwing business their way, so it's a two-way favor. Be sure to tell the banker that you've checked out the buyer financially, because this will help you get an early appointment.

The first bank to talk to is the bank that holds your mortgage. They should be willing to loan on the house because they have the most to gain. Their yield on the loan could go up. Their processing fees will go down. And if they wrote your loan at a low interest rate, they will have the opportunity to raise the interest earned on your remaining principal.

VA/FHA MORTGAGES

It used to be that people were somewhat reluctant to sell to buyers using VA/FHA or other government mortgages. One reason was that the seller was required to pay the discount points. That's been made optional on FHA loans, and on VA loans the points have been reduced, easing resistance to such mortgages. Another reason was that people thought they had to do extensive work to sell VA/FHA, but that really isn't true, either. Nowadays, such mortgages involve about the same amount of effort as loans from conventional lenders. If you want to offer your house VA/FHA— and advertise it as such—go ahead. Just figure the points you pay into your price (make certain that VA/FHA lends in your specific area, as there may be some local restrictions).

ASSUMABLE MORTGAGES

Ask your banker whether your loan can be assumed and, if so, on what terms. It could benefit both you and your buyer and thus could be a selling point. Assuming your mortgage could, for example, save weeks in the closing time and reduce your buyer's closing costs. It may also lower the overall interest rate your buyer pays.

The important concern with an assumable mortgage is to protect yourself from future liability.

Generally, there are two ways your buyer can take over your mortgage. One method is to purchase the property "subject to" the existing morgage. The buyer must of course make the monthly mortgage payments or lose the property by foreclosure. But the buyer has no liability, because he or she didn't assume the loan payment obligation. You still are liable if the lender has to foreclose and suffers a loss in the process.

One variation of buying subject to an assumable mortgage includes a no-money-down aspect and should be regarded carefully. If your buyer can't qualify for his or her own mortgage, he or she may ask you to refinance the house yourself, take whatever net cash you get from the deal, and accept the buyer's note for the remainder of the price and his or her promise to take over your mortgage. The trick is, if the buyer doesn't make the mortgage payments, you will still be liable for repaying the bank. A buyer can't assume liability for your mortgage without passing a credit check.

On top of it all, if you try to sell the note you received for your equity, you may be offered 50 percent or less of its face value. The result is you lose money.

The second, and preferred, method is for the buyer to assume the existing mortgage and the loan payment obligation. Be certain the lender releases you from further liability if your buyer assumes your mortgage. If the lender doesn't—and lenders have been known to "neglect" to release the seller from liability on the assumed mortgage—the lender can go after you if there's a foreclosure loss and they can't collect from your assuming buyer. In practice, foreclosure losses rarely occur and commercial lenders seldom go after deficiency judgments. Nevertheless, it does happen with FHA and VA mortgages where the government actively pursues foreclosure deficiency losses.

SELLER FINANCING: THE NO-MONEY-DOWN DEAL

If you agree to a no-money-down deal, you are basically accepting a piece of paper—a promissory note—for your equity instead of demanding cash.

Is such a deal for you? Rarely. No-money-down deals work best when you own most or all of the property free and clear. Even then, they may not be in your best interest.

For a seller the attraction of engaging in a no-money-down deal is getting the full asking price. Such greed is the opening the no-cash buyer is looking for. He or she steps in and offers your asking price. On paper, it looks like a good deal.

But no-cash sales can be just price cuts by another name. The value of that money you agree to accept in the future will be eroded by inflation, especially if you are getting anything less than the going interest rate for long-term investments. Most of the time, you're better off cutting the price up front and taking your cash, rather than going for a richer deal that could turn out to be pie in the sky.

If you're considering offering a no-money-down deal to sweeten the package, consider your own motives. Is the price too high to attract a conventionally financed buyer? If you lowered the price, could you attract a conventional buyer?

If you still think a no-money-down deal can be to your advantage, tread cautiously and consider your buyer's financial position carefully. The deal can carry additional risk. Ask some questions:

- What's the buyer's financial position? (Don't just take his word for it.)
- Does he have the income and savings to buy your house on normal terms? Or is her savings tied up, leaving no cash cushion for you?
- Is his credit good?
- How many loans does he have already outstanding? Maybe he has defaulted on a real estate deal.
- If her credit isn't good enough for a bank to deal with her, is it good enough for you to do so?
- Why wouldn't the bank loan to her? Is it because she's likely to default?
- Is the buyer's investment plan sound?
- If he buys the house as an investment and pays the asking price, will the rent payments cover his costs? If not, where will he get the difference?
- Will he eventually stop making payments to you and force you to go through the legal hassles to get your money out of him?
- What will you do if she falls behind in payments and asks to renegotiate the deal on terms that effectively reduce the price? Will you feel forced to accept, because of the cost and uncertainties of foreclosing?
- Will he mortgage the house when you deed it to him, give you a bit of the cash, and use the rest for something else? If he then walks away from the bank mortgage, the bank will foreclose. You'd have to make the bank whole again to get your property back and protect your equity.

If the bank won't give the buyer a mortgage without a down payment, he or she may try to fake it, and ask you to help. Be warned: It's a federal offense to lie to a federally insured financial institution.

Generally, however, regardless of the type of financing your buyer uses, you should be willing and ready to help in the process because it serves your interest. At the very least, seek information on the time involved in getting a mortgage loan in your area because it will help you in planning your own timetable for moving or buying your next house.

10
The Title and
the Survey

After the contract has been signed, a number of details have to be taken care of. Your title to the property must be examined. The property must be surveyed. The premises must be inspected.

Typically, your lawyer will intercede for you in all the aspects of the transaction relating to your property's title, title search, and title insurance. Indeed, this aspect of the sale involves legal steps that must be taken to protect the buyer. As seller, though, it is a good idea for you to know what will be expected of you in documenting the ownership of your house.

Chances are the buyer will ask for a new survey of your property unless, for some reason, you have ordered a survey done in the past six months. The new survey will cost you between $50 and $100, depending on local rates. Your lawyer usually will arrange for the survey.

TITLE SEARCH

Next, or perhaps simultaneously, your lawyer will arrange for a title search. The search is typically performed by a local title company, though in some regions only practicing attorneys can perform it. That process will cost quite a bit more than a survey. Depending on your market, a title search can cost between $500 and $1,000. Besides your legal fee, the title search will be the most expensive part of selling your house. But it is also an absolutely essential part of the sale.

As title insurance executives point out, a title is a bundle of rights in real property. A title search, simply put, determines that the person who is selling the property really has the rights to sell it, and that the buyer is getting all the rights to the property that he or she is paying for.

Some of the questions a title search covers are:

- Are all taxes and special assessments paid?
- Does anyone have special rights to the property that would limit the buyer's ownership?
- Has the death of a former owner or the filing of a will affected title to the property?
- If there is an abstract (history) of the title, is the abstract complete, and does it reveal all defects in the title?
- Are there undisclosed heirs?

A public record search will uncover most of the problems that can arise with title claims. But in the majority of real estate transactions, the seller purchases a title insurance policy to assure the buyer that the title purchased is valid. In those transactions, the title company must determine the "insurability" of the title as part of the search process.

The insurance company then issues a title policy, which insures the existence or lack of rights to the property and binds the insurance company to pay losses incurred due to any challenge to the title. If a claim is made against the insured's title, the title insurance company will defend the title in court, if necessary. The insurance company bears the court costs, as well as the cost of settling the claim if it proves valid, in order to protect your title and keep you in possession of the property. More importantly, the title insurer fills a preventive role in a real estate transaction.

Title insurance assures that every possible cloud over the title to the property that is being purchased has been called to the buyer's attention, so that any defects can be corrected before the transaction takes place.

Here's what the title company will discover in its title search:

- *Chain of title*—This is simply a history of the ownership of your house and surrounding property. This documentation is derived either from a county clerk's or recorder's office, or from title plants privately owned and maintained by the title companies.
- *Tax search*—This search reveals whether taxes are current or past due and unpaid from previous years. It also indicates whether any special assessments exist against the property and whether the assessments are current or past due. A buyer who purchases a property with unpaid and past-due taxes or assessments against it could be confronted by town, county, or state officials who want to sell the house for payment of the taxes and assessments. Title insurance protects the buyer against such losses, but the tax search really is the best protection of all for the buyer.
- *Report on possession*—In most cases, particularly when one of the dozen or so major title insurance companies is involved, the title company will send an inspector to the property to verify the lot size and the location of improvements, such as fences, swimming pools, or a garage, as well as to check on who is living there. The inspection supplements the information collected from the title search. If the inspector detects an unrecorded easement or other evidence of outstanding rights that could affect the buyer's title and possibly the value and intended use, the title company tells the buyer of these things before the sale is closed. These matters then become issues to be settled between buyer and seller, or must be listed as exceptions in the title insurance

policy. Sometimes—quite often, in fact—when an acceptable survey and appropriate affidavits are received, an inspection will not be made.

- *Judgment and name search*—Finally, the title search should uncover any unsatisfied judgment against the seller or previous owners that existed when they owned the property's title. A judgment is a lien against the debtor's real estate and constitutes security for any money owed under the judgment. Indeed, the real estate can be sold to satisfy the judgment. Because a judgment can exist against someone with the same name as yours and thus be mistakenly applied to your property, a name search is also done as part of the judgment search.

HIDDEN RISKS

These procedures protect you and the buyer from 90 percent of the legal hang-ups that can arise with the transfer of property titles. But the reason you probably bought title insurance when you purchased your house, and the reason your buyer will, is for protection from the hidden risks of buying property.

While these risks are rare, all homeowners should be aware of them:

- The seller can be divorced (or secretly married) in another state, with a spouse or former spouse who may have a claim against the seller.
- The person who sold you your house can have heirs who may not have been known to them, but who may bring a claim against the new owners if the seller later dies. This can happen in cases where the seller dies without a will or when a will is contested.
- The owner may have been fraudulently impersonated. Deeds, releases, mortgages, or other documents may be forgeries.
- A deed may have been delivered to a buyer without the owner's consent, as in a son or daughter selling

elderly parents' property, or it may be transferred after a power of attorney has expired.

- Clerical errors, though unusual, can also cause title problems later for a buyer.

CONDOMINIUM TITLES

If the sale involves a condominium, the process will be like that for a single-family house. When you buy a condominium unit, you acquire individual and absolute title to the space your unit occupies. You also own an undivided interest—collectively with all other unit owners in the condominium—in the common areas of the building, such as the stairs, hallways, main walls, roofs, lobbies, and surrounding land used jointly by all owners.

You are buying title to a cube of space, but in spite of its intangible nature, a condominium's air space is treated under the law just like a piece of land. So all of the procedures for a single-family house will be used to perform a title search on a condominium and the land on which the building stands.

Additionally, the individual unit must be described by dividing, measuring, and locating it three-dimensionally so that it cannot possibly be confused with any other unit space.

INSURANCE COMMITMENT

When all searches are complete, the title insurance company issues a "commitment to insure," stating the conditions under which it will insure the title. If any defects are found in the title, the seller must clear them up before the title of the new buyer can be issued free and clear.

Your buyer's lender is as concerned as the buyer about the quality of the title. All mortgage lenders buy title insurance in the amount of the mortgage. That policy is separate from the one the buyer purchases.

There is no law that dictates who picks the title company. Different traditions have developed in different regions of the country. In some states, the mortgage lender will hire the title insurance company for both the buyer and itself. In other states, the seller's lawyer may select the title insurer, and in still other states, the real estate broker selects the title company.

It is important to note that the mortgage lender's policy is written to protect the lender from any later claims against the title's validity. The buyer's policy is to protect the buyer from such claims. Both policies—the lender's and the buyer's—are necessary for a safe title transfer. While the lender's and the buyer's title policies protect separate interests, they are linked in another way. If the mortgage policy and homeowner's policy are issued at the same time, then the buyer's cost for a second policy is minimal.

The seller typically pays for the title search. A rule of thumb is that the cost of title search and insurance amounts to about 0.5 percent of the sale price of your house. The seller will pay for the title search and the updated property survey, while the buyer pays for the title insurance.

Chapter 12 explains how all these documents are finally processed by the lender, the title company, the seller, the buyer, and the attorneys.

11
The Appraisal

While some sellers may opt for hiring an appraiser before they set their asking price, most sellers will meet their first appraiser when their buyer's mortgage lender orders an appraisal.

The purpose of the appraisal is to get an expert opinion of your property's value. It assures the mortgage lender that in the rare event of a default, it would be able to get most if not all of its money back by selling the property.

As a seller, you may be a bit anxious at the prospect of an appraisal. What if the appraiser comes in with a price far below the price you've agreed to with your buyer? Even more dreadful, what if the appraiser comes in with a much higher value than the one on the sales contract? Will you find out you're giving your property away?

As interest rates fluctuate more dramatically than ever before, and as rehabilitation of many city neighborhoods changes the value of property (almost overnight in some cases), appraisals have become less predictable and appraisers have come under fire for not doing a thorough job of analyzing a property. As mentioned earlier, you will probably have no say in who will perform the appraisal. In nearly all real estate transactions, the appraiser will be selected by the mortgage lender.

FINDING AN APPRAISER

In seller-financed deals, you and your lawyer will be responsible for finding an appraiser. If you are, look for members of the American Institute of Real Estate Appraisers. They are listed in a directory published by the American Institute of Real Estate Appraisers every January. The institute's directory is available by writing to:

American Institute of Real Estate Appraisers
430 N. Michigan Avenue
Chicago, Ill. 60611-4088
(312) 329-8559

Locally, institute members will publish MAI (Member, Appraisal Institute) or RM (Residential Member) after their names in the telephone directory. If you are financing the sale and are responsible for finding an appraiser, your lawyer may be the best source for referral, particularly if the lawyer does a great deal of real estate work.

In any event, a member of the appraisal institute is worth finding. Though membership is no guarantee, at least you know your appraiser has had specialized training in appraisal work, is aware of industry-enforced codes of ethics and standards of professional practice, and has received professional recognition for mastery of the institute's educational program.

HOW AN APPRAISER DOES THE JOB

Appraisers, it is important to understand, give an expert *opinion* of what a property is worth. They do not determine a property's value.

The appraiser uses one of these methods to value property:

1. The value indicated by recent sales of comparable properties in the market
2. The value that the property's net earning power will support
3. The current cost of reproducing or replacing a building, minus an estimate for depreciation, plus the value of the land

The first method, called a sales comparison, is always used for residential real estate appraisals. The second method is used on income-producing properties, and the final method is usually used for insurance purposes.

When an appraiser does a sales comparison, he or she researches the market within about one mile of your house. The appraiser gets information about transactions, listings, and other offerings of properties similar to yours. He or she verifies this information with a knowledgeable source to check that the data are accurate and that the transactions with which yours is compared reflect arm's-length market considerations.

Finally, the appraiser determines relevant units of comparison—square feet if your property is a single-family home or condominium, or acreage if your property is, say, a ranch—and develops a comparative analysis for each unit. He or she compares your property to comparable sales and adjusts the sale price of each comparable as appropriate or eliminates the property as a comparable. He or she reconciles the several value indications that result from the comparables into a single valuation.

Appraisal requires a great deal of judgment even after all the numbers have been crunched. It is an inexact science because so many variables can affect a house's price. In general, however, elements of comparison include the following:

- Financing
- Conditions of sale
- Market conditions
- Location

- Physical characteristics
- Income characteristics, if the property includes rental units

Other Appraisal Approaches

We have detailed the sales comparison appraisal because it is the approach most often used for single-family houses. If your home happens to be a two-flat or duplex, you may have an appraisal based on income capitalization. Briefly, capitalization begins with an estimate of net operating income, from which the appraiser develops a rate of capitalization and estimates the property's value.

The third method of appraisal, the cost approach, is used almost exclusively to determine insurable value.

The Appraisal Report

The form, length, and content of an appraisal report depend on the type of property covered. However, the American Institute of Real Estate Appraisers has set some standards for what should be included in an appraiser's report.

As a seller, you probably will not see the appraisal, as long as it satisfies the buyer and the mortgage lender. However, you may request through your lawyer a copy of the appraisal if it comes in below your contract price and buyer's remorse sets in on your once-enthusiastic buyer. An appraiser is required to defend every aspect of the report and justify all of the comparables.

If the appraisal comes in lower than the sales price, you may consider yielding on your price, say meeting your buyer halfway on the difference, if it means keeping the deal alive.

THE APPRAISAL APPOINTMENT

If you were using a real estate broker, he or she would probably make a point of being present when the appraiser tours your house. So, you will have to do that yourself. The appraiser will tell what he or she has to see, so you should not have to say much unless he or she leaves a major feature out of the inspection, such as an extra bath, the garage, or a finished basement.

Make sure your house is clean, the yard trimmed, and the front lawn mowed. Appraisers, like prospects, are impressed, however subliminally, by cleanliness and curb appeal.

12
Closing/Settlement

The closing, or settlement as it is called in some parts of the country, is the final step in the sale of your house. It is the formal process by which the title of the property passes from you to your buyer and money passes from your buyer to you.

It can occur any time from two weeks to two months after you actually sign the sales contract, depending on how busy the lenders, appraisers, and loan processors are and what kind of financing your buyer secured. When closing does arrive, you are committed to the sale of your property and, unless your buyer has failed to perform a legally binding promise or has acted fraudulently, you are normally obligated to complete your part of the contract. By this time, any changes in settlement costs and purchase terms may be extremely difficult to negotiate. So, be sure everything is in order from your point of view.

No standard closing process is followed in all parts of the country. Settlements may be conducted by lending institutions, title insurance companies, escrow companies, real estate brokers, or attorneys for the buyer or the seller. They do, however, generally use a standard form, called a

Uniform Settlement Statement, to itemize the financial details of the closing.

In some areas, an actual meeting will take place between you, your buyer, your respective lawyers, and the closing agent. In other areas, there is no meeting at all. In such cases, the person conducting the closing has the obligation to deliver the Uniform Settlement Statement to you by mail. Check with your lawyer to learn local custom and practice.

SHOPPING FOR SERVICES

Generally, it falls to the buyer to shop for providers of closing services, because the buyer pays the bulk of closing costs. Your broker, if you had one, would help your buyer by recommending services. You can do the same, but first find out whether your help is necessary.

Some lending institutions designate specific providers of settlement services to be used for legal services, title examination services, title insurance, or the conduct of settlement. When this happens, the lender is required to provide your buyer with good-faith estimates of the cost of such services and a statement in which the lender identifies the providers by name and tells whether each designated firm has a business relationship with the lender. The suggested settlement agent may not be the least expensive, and you might save money by taking the initiative to arrange for settlement and select the firm and location that meets your needs.

CLOSING COSTS

Along with being the time to swap property title for money, closing is also the time to pay certain charges and fees that occur in connection with the sale of your house. These fees are known as closing costs or settlement charges. Depending on the deal you cut with your buyer, you may pay all closing costs, part of them, or none of them. Though some may be negotiable practically up to the time of closing, you generally should be responsible for the fees settled in the sales contract. For exact amounts, consult with your attorney or the closing agent, who should give you (or your attorney) itemized costs at least the day before closing.

As closing procedures vary from area to area, so do closing costs and services. The settlement charges that are usually levied include:

- Sales/broker's commission
- Items payable in connection with the loan
- Items required by lender to be paid in advance
- Reserves deposited with the lender
- Title charges
- Government recording and transfer charges
- Additional settlement charges

Sales Commission

The sales commission can be the largest fee charged at closing, but you won't pay any. If your buyer employed a broker, let your buyer pay for it.

Items Payable in Connection with the Loan

The items payable in connection with the loan include the following:

- The loan origination fee, which covers the lender's administrative costs of loan processing, and usually is paid by the buyer
- The appraisal fee, which pays for a statement of property value for the lender, and may be paid by either the buyer or the seller
- The credit report fee, which covers the cost of the credit report on the buyer, and usually is paid for by the buyer.
- The lender's inspection fee, which covers the cost of inspections made by bank or outside inspectors, and is usually paid for by the buyer
- The mortgage insurance application fee, which

covers processing application for private mortgage insurance, which is required on certain loans
- The assumption fee, which covers processing papers for cases in which the buyer takes over payments on the prior loan of the seller

Items Required by Lender to Be Paid in Advance

The lender requires certain items to be paid in advance. These items are customarily paid by the buyer. They include the following:

- Interest that accrues on the mortgage from the date of the settlement to the beginning of the period covered by the first monthly payment
- The first premium on mortgage insurance, which protects the lender from loss due to payment default by the new homeowner
- The first premium for hazard insurance, which protects both buyer and lender against loss due to fire, windstorm, and other natural hazards

Reserves Deposited with Lender

The reserves deposited with the lender are customarily paid by the buyer (as the borrower) and placed in escrow or impound accounts. They are funds held in account by the lender to assure future payment for such recurring items as real estate taxes, hazard insurance, mortgage insurance, property taxes, and annual or special assessments.

Title Charges

Title charges may cover a variety of fees for services involved in the closing transaction, with different settlement items applying to different areas. In general, they include the fees that follow:

- The settlement fee paid to the settlement agent,

usually negotiated in the sales contract between buyer and seller

- The title search, examination, and insurance binder, which basically certify that you are passing clear title to your buyer and that, if a binder has been issued, a title insurance company has committed to insuring the title
- The document preparation fee, which covers the preparation of legal papers, such as mortgage, deed, etc. (find out whether these fees are covered under some other service—ask the settlement agent or your lawyer)
- The notary fee, which covers the cost of a licensed person affixing a seal to the various documents that need authentication
- Attorney's fees for services provided to the lender in connection with the settlement—usually paid by the buyer, though sometimes shared by the seller
- Title insurance, of which you may pay all, part, or none, depending on the terms of the sales contract
- Lender's title insurance, which protects the lender against defects in the title, for which a one-time premium may be charged at settlement and for which the buyer customarily pays
- Owner's title insurance, which protects your buyer against defects in the title, and for which you usually pay; in some areas, if your buyer wants it, he or she has to pay for it

Government Recording and Transfer Charges

Government recording and transfer charges are collected for recording the new deed and mortgage. They may include purchasing state tax stamps and may be substantial. These items are negotiable in the sales contract, but the buyer usually pays the fees for the new deed and the mortgage. Be careful that you don't get stuck on this. Consult your lawyer.

Additional Settlement Charges

Additional settlement charges vary from locale to locale but may include the following ones:

- Survey fees for a property survey to determine the exact location of the house and the lot line, as well as easements and rights of way. Usually the buyer pays the surveyor's fees, but they also may be handled by the seller.
- Inspection fees, for insects or perhaps other types of inspections. These are usually paid by the buyer.

SAMPLE WORKSHEET

Now that you understand what the various closing costs are likely to be, take a look at the following worksheet. It was taken from an actual HUD Uniform Settlement Statement and will help you itemize and total the closing costs you may be liable for, depending on what is negotiated in the sales contract.

CALCULATING YOUR PROFIT

Once you know what your closing costs will be, you can begin to calculate your profit from the sale of your house. There are three factors to consider:

1. Gross amount due you
2. Reductions in the amount due you
3. Cash to you

Gross Amount Due You

The gross due you includes the contract sales price, which is the price agreed to in the sales contract, and payment for any personal property that will be transferred with the house, if a separate bargain was struck for it. Items of personal property may include carpets, drapes, stove, and other appliances.

SETTLEMENT CHARGES WORKSHEET

	Paid From Borrower's Funds at Settlement	Paid From Seller's Funds at Settlement
700. **TOTAL SALES/BROKER'S COMMISSION** based on price $ _____ @ _____ % =		
Division of Commission (line 700) as follows:		
701. $ _____ to		
702. $ _____ to		
703. Commission paid at Settlement		
704.		
800. **ITEMS PAYABLE IN CONNECTION WITH LOAN**		
801. Loan Origination Fee _____ %		
802. Loan Discount _____ %		
803. Appraisal Fee to		
804. Credit Report to		
805. Lender's Inspection Fee		
806. Mortgage Insurance Application Fee to		
807. Assumption Fee		
808.		
809.		
810.		
811.		
900. **ITEMS REQUIRED BY LENDER TO BE PAID IN ADVANCE**		
901. Interest from _____ to _____ @ $ _____ /day		
902. Mortgage Insurance Premium for _____ months to		
903. Hazard Insurance Premium for _____ years to		
904. _____ years to		
905.		
1000. **RESERVES DEPOSITED WITH LENDER**		
1001. Hazard insurance _____ months @ $ _____ per month		
1002. Mortgage insurance _____ months @ $ _____ per month		
1003. City property taxes _____ months @ $ _____ per month		
1004. County property taxes _____ months @ $ _____ per month		
1005. Annual assessments _____ months @ $ _____ per month		
1006. _____ months @ $ _____ per month		
1007. _____ months @ $ _____ per month		
1008. _____ months @ $ _____ per month		
1100. **TITLE CHARGES**		
1101. Settlement or closing fee to		
1102. Abstract or title search to		
1103. Title examination to		
1104. Title insurance binder to		
1105. Document preparation to		
1106. Notary fees to		
1107. Attorney's fees to		
(includes above items numbers; _____)		
1108. Title insurance to		
(includes above items numbers; _____)		
1109. Lender's coverage $		
1110. Owner's coverage $		
1111.		
1112.		
1113.		
1200. **GOVERNMENT RECORDING AND TRANSFER CHARGES**		
1201. Recording fees: Deed $ _____ ; Mortgage $ _____ ; Releases $		
1202. City/county tax/stamps: Deed $ _____ ; Mortgage $		
1203. State tax/stamps: Deed $ _____ ; Mortgage $		
1204.		
1205.		
1300. **ADDITIONAL SETTLEMENT CHARGES**		
1301. Survey to		
1302. Pest inspection to		
1303.		
1304.		
1305.		
1400. **TOTAL SETTLEMENT CHARGES** (enter on lines 103, Section J and 502, Section K):		

The category also includes "adjustments for items paid by seller in advance." These include refunds on taxes, footage charges, insurance, rent, fuel, and other items that you have previously paid for covering a time beyond the settlement date. To calculate these amounts you will need to use the prorating table shown here. At the bottom of the table are examples that illustrate how to use the table.

Reductions in Amount Due You

Reductions in amount due you include any excess deposits (such as earnest money) that you have to give back to the buyer, settlement charges that you've agreed to pay, and payment of the balance on your existing mortgage and on a second mortgage if you have one. Others may include any taxes or assessments that are due after settlement, but which you agree to pay because they cover a period of time before settlement. Money for such items may be held in a reserve account. For the balance on your existing mortgage, the title company will cut a check and either mail it to your lender or give it to your lawyer to mail.

Cash to You

Cash to you is the difference between the gross amount due you and the reductions in the amount due you.

Now that you understand the factors involved, you can calculate your profit on the cash-to-seller worksheet that follows, which is taken from a HUD Settlement Statement.

COMMISSION AS PROFIT—WHAT YOU'VE SAVED

When you have figured your net profit from the deal, you can subtract what the broker's fee would have been for the sale of your house to figure just how well you did. For example, say you sold your house for $100,000. Sales

PRORATING TABLE

Number of years, months and days	RENTS One Month — Days to Month		TAXES & INS. — One Year		INSURANCE — Three Years			Five Years			Number of years months and days
	30	31	Months	Days	Years	Months	Days	Years	Months	Days	
1	.0333	.0323	.0833	.0028	.3333	.0278	.0009	.2000	.0167	.0006	1
2	.0667	.0645	.1667	.0056	.6667	.0556	.0019	.4000	.0333	.0011	2
3	.1000	.0968	.2500	.0083	1.0000	.0833	.0028	.6000	.0500	.0017	3
4	.1333	.1290	.3333	.0111		.1111	.0037	.8000	.0667	.0022	4
5	.1667	.1613	.4167	.0139		.1389	.0046	1.0000	.0833	.0028	5
6	.2000	.1935	.5000	.0167		.1667	.0056		.1000	.0033	6
7	.2333	.2258	.5833	.0194		.1944	.0065		.1167	.0039	7
8	.2667	.2581	.6667	.0222		.2222	.0074		.1333	.0044	8
9	.3000	.2903	.7500	.0250		.2500	.0083		.1500	.0050	9
10	.3333	.3226	.8333	.0278		.2778	.0093		.1667	.0056	10
11	.3667	.3548	.9167	.0306		.3056	.0102		.1833	.0061	11
12	.4000	.3871	1.0000	.0333		.3333	.0111		.2000	.0067	12
13	.4333	.4194		.0361			.0120			.0072	13
14	.4667	.4516		.0389			.0130			.0078	14
15	.5000	.4839		.0417			.0139			.0083	15
16	.5333	.5161		.0444			.0148			.0089	16
17	.5667	.5484		.0472			.0157			.0094	17
18	.6000	.5806		.0500			.0167			.0100	18
19	.6333	.6129		.0528			.0176			.0106	19
20	.6667	.6452		.0556			.0185			.0111	20
21	.7000	.6774		.0583			.0194			.0117	21
22	.7333	.7097		.0611			.0204			.0122	22
23	.7667	.7419		.0639			.0213			.0128	23
24	.8000	.7742		.0667			.0222			.0133	24
25	.8333	.8065		.0694			.0231			.0139	25
26	.8667	.8387		.0722			.0241			.0144	26
27	.9000	.8710		.0750			.0250			.0150	27
28	.9333	.9032		.0778			.0259			.0156	28
29	.9667	.9355		.0806			.0269			.0161	29
30	1.0000	.9677		.0833			.0278			.0167	30
31		1.0000									31

Example
nt $135.00 per mo.
find value of 23
ys of a 31 day mo.
om Table: —
days =
19 x 135.00 =   .7419
0.16

Example
Taxes =   1215.12,
To find value of 7 mos. and 19 days
From Table: —
7 mos. =   .5833
19 days =   .0528
7 mos. 19 days =   .6361
.6361 x 1215.12 =

Example
3 Year Policy Premium = 58.75
To find the value of 1 yr. 3 mos. 11 days
From Table: —
1 yr. =   .3333
3 mos. =   .0833
11 days =   .0102
1 yr. 3 mo. 11 days =   .4268
.4268 x 58.75 = 25.07

Example
5 Yr. Policy Premium = 312.82
To find value of 3 yrs. mos. 13 days
From Table: —
3 yrs. =   .6000
4 mos. =   .0667
13 days =   .0072
3 yrs. 4 mo. 13 days =   .6739
.6739 x 312.82 = 210.81

CASH-TO-SELLER WORKSHEET

400.	**GROSS AMOUNT DUE TO SELLER:**
401.	Contract sales price
402.	Personal property
403.	
404.	
405.	

Adjustments for items paid by seller in advance

406.	City/town taxes	to
407.	County taxes	to
408.	Assessments	to
409.		
410.		
411.		
412.		
420.	**GROSS AMOUNT DUE TO SELLER**	

500.	**REDUCTIONS IN AMOUNT DUE TO SELLER:**
501.	Excess deposit *(see instructions)*
502.	Settlement charges to seller *(line 1400)*
503.	Existing loan(s) taken subject to
504.	Payoff of first mortgage loan
505.	Payoff of second mortgage loan
506.	
507.	
508.	
509.	

Adjustments for items unpaid by seller

510.	City/town taxes	to
511.	County taxes	to
512	Assessments	to
513.		
514.		
515.		
516.		
517.		
518.		
519.		
520.	**TOTAL REDUCTION AMOUNT DUE SELLER**	

600.	**CASH AT SETTLEMENT TO/FROM SELLER**
601.	Gross amount due to seller *(line 420)*
602.	Less reductions in amount due seller *(line 520)* ( )
603.	**CASH (☐ TO) (☐ FROM) SELLER**

commission, at 6 percent of the sales price, would have been $6,000. Now, say you netted $40,000 (cash to you at closing) on the house. That $6,000 commission would have reduced your net profit to $34,000—or 15 percent of your profit, not just 6 percent of the sales price. This amount is what you've saved by selling your house without a broker.

Index

Mortgage insurance, 85–86
Multiple-listing form. *See* Property description fact sheet

Negotiating sale, 38–39
No-money-down
 and assumable mortgage, 68
 and seller financing, 70–71
Notary fee, 87

Offer, 8, 35, 37
Outbuildings, 26
Owner financing, 29

PITI (principal, interest, tax, insurance), 41–42
Plumbing, 34, 64
Preparing house. *See* Home improvements
Pricing strategy, 3, 5, 15–16
Promissory note, 69
Property description fact sheet, 35, 36
Property survey, 22
Property tax bill, 22
Property taxes. *See* Taxes
Prorating table, 90, 91
Prospect
 prequalifying, 29
 screening, 29
 enticing to inspect house, 29–30
 defining, 30

Qualifying buyer, 37–53
 bank's qualification rules, 40
 confidentiality, 40
 and PITI, 41–42
 process, 40–41
 timing, 40

Real estate broker. *See* Broker
Real estate taxes. *See* Taxes
Realtor. *See* Broker
Rehabilitated property, 14
Report on possession, 74–75
Reserves deposited with lender, 86
Residential loan application, 45, 50–53
RM (Residential Member), 79
Room dimensions, 34

Sales agreement. *See* Contract of sale
Sales contract, 21, 38, 39
Sales commission. *See* Broker sales commission
Sales comparison method, 80–81
Schools, proximity to, 26
Second mortgage, 90
Seller financing, 66, 69–71
Seller's market, 23
Selling techniques, 35
Selling without a broker, odds, 6
Selling without a broker, trial period, 6–7
Setting price of house, 12–16
Settlement charges worksheet, 89
Settlement costs. *See* Closing costs
Settlement fee, 86–87
Shopping, proximity to, 26
Showing the house, 33–34
Siding, 26
Society of Real Estate Appraisers, 13
"Subject to" an assumable mortgage, 68
Survey, 61, 72
Survey fees, 88